KANT ON HISTORY

The Library of Liberal Arts
OSKAR PIEST, FOUNDER

ON HISTORY

IMMANUEL KANT

Edited, with an introduction, by
LEWIS WHITE BECK

Translated by
LEWIS WHITE BECK
ROBERT E. ANCHOR
and
EMIL L. FACKENHEIM

The Library of Liberal Arts
published by

Macmillan Publishing Company
New York
Collier Macmillan Publishers
London

Immanuel Kant: 1724-1804

CONTENTS
· · · · · · · · · · · · · · · ·

ON HISTORY

EDITOR'S INTRODUCTION

Immanuel Kant was not a historian. In his literary remains, we find this note: "I shall not make my head into a parchment and scribble old, half-effaced information from archives on it." He was a philosopher, with a philosophy that seems singularly unlikely to encourage a philosopher to take history seriously. His *Critique of Pure Reason* studied the foundations of knowledge; but by "knowledge" he meant almost exclusively Newtonian physics, and by "foundations" he meant unchanging a priori forms and categories of the mind. His *Critique of Practical Reason* studied the foundations of ethics; but from them everything anthropological, having to do with the varieties of human natures and circumstance, and everything historical, concerning the development of moral codes and institutions, was ruled out as irrelevant and even dangerous in the study of morals. The intelligible world under universal moral law and the world of nature under universal causal law seem the upper and nether millstones of this philosophy, between which all life would be crushed out of history.

Yet he did have a philosophy of history. His writings on history began in the period between these two great *Critiques,* and they seem oddly out of place. Stylistically the first ones seem to belong in the period two decades earlier when he wrote such popular works as *Observations on the Feelings of the Beautiful and the Sublime* and the *Dreams of a Spirit-Seer.* Like them, the early papers on history are graceful, ironic, even whimsical at times; but they were written in the period when his other works were severely scholastic in style and forbiddingly difficult in content.

Because of this contrast in style and material, the writings on history have sometimes been seen as hardly more than expressions of Kant's personal interest in historical narratives and his enthusiasm for freedom of the press, freedom of re-

ligion, peace among nations, and republican government. As
such they have been repeatedly set over against his "official
philosophy," and either studied in isolation or neglected altogether.

But is such a sharp cleavage really credible? Remember that
Kant in 1784, the date of the earliest essay in this book, was
sixty years old (and felt much older); that the working out of
his system was a challenge he feared he might not live to meet;
and that he and his disciples were then involved in disagree-
able polemics that showed him that he had not yet succeeded
in making his new philosophy intelligible and acceptable, so
that work already done had to be done again. Is it not more
likely, then, that this busy and hurried man saw his writings
on history in some more intimate connection with the main
body of his life work than many of his interpreters have found?
What might this connection be?

II

Kant's writings on the philosophy of history began to appear
in 1784. In November and December of that year he published
two essays, "What is Enlightenment?" and "Idea for a Universal History from a Cosmopolitan Point of View," in the *Berlinische Monatsschrift,* one of the chief organs of the German
Enlightenment, edited by his friend Biester. He explained the
occasion for the writing of the second of these essays in the
note given below (p. 11).

In July of the same year, Schütz, another friend and disciple,
had invited him to review the just published Part One of Herder's *Ideas for a Philosophy of the History of Mankind* in the
Allgemeine Literaturzeitung of Jena. Kant agreed, but with
some hesitation and an offer to relinquish the honorarium
should his review not seem suitable. His hesitancy, perhaps,
was a consequence of the chill that had come over the earlier
warm relations between him and Herder. Johann Gottfried
Herder had been a pupil of Kant's in 1762-64; but philosophically they were far apart, with Herder leading the *Sturm und*

Drang opposition to academic philosophy and "Kantian rationalism." Though they did not see each other again after the early days in Königsberg, there was a brief but friendly correspondence; then their opposition hardened, no doubt partly under the influence of meddling friends like Johann Georg Hamann, Kant's neighbor and Herder's mentor.

The review, published anonymously in January, 1785, was mainly expository and by the standards of the time a mild one. But Herder was deeply offended, exclaiming bitterly, "I am forty years old and no longer a pupil sitting on his metaphysical school-bench."[1] Karl Leonhard Reinhold, a friend of Herder, replied to the review, and Kant wrote a rejoinder (below, p. 40) which was published in the March number.[2] In November of the same year, Kant reviewed Part Two of the *Ideas.* Though he was again complaining of lack of time, this Part had contained an attack on Kant's "Idea for a Universal History" and Kant replied in self-defense. But he declined to review the remaining parts of the *Ideas* as they were published.

He was not, however, done with Herder, and in 1786 he invaded Herder's own territory with one of the most unusual essays he ever wrote: "Conjectural Beginning of Human History," published in the *Berlinische Monatsschrift.* Years earlier, in an essay entitled "The Most Ancient Document of the Human Race," and again in his *Ideas,* Part Two, Herder had given his interpretation of the book of Genesis. Kant, in his turn, showed how the book of Genesis could be read in the light of *his* philosophy of history. The essay is, as it were, an allegory based on the first two chapters of Genesis and on the third thesis of his "Idea for a Universal History": "Nature has willed that man should, by himself, produce everything that

1 Quoted from K. Vorländer, *Immanuel Kant, der Mann und das Werk* (Leipzig, 1924), I, 319-20.
2 Shortly thereafter Reinhold changed his allegiance and became one of Kant's most influential disciples. Though Herder's opposition to Kant's philosophy continued to grow throughout his life and later led him to write two books explicitly directed against Kant, his recollection of Kant published in 1792 (see below, p. xxviii) gives one of the most sympathetic portraits we have of Kant's character and personality.

goes beyond the mechanical ordering of his animal existence, and that he should partake of no other happiness or perfection than that which he himself, independently of instinct, has created by his own reason."

In "The End of All Things," published in the *Berlinische Monatsschrift* in 1794, Kant turned his attention from the beginning of human history to its end. This essay, which he said was to be read "partly as doleful, partly as droll," [3] discussed the apocalyptic doctrine of the end of the world. After showing that eschatology lies beyond the scope of theoretical or speculative reason, he pointed to the moral significance (and moral dangers) in the doctrine of the Last Judgment. In the concluding section, he contrasted Christianity, which he interpreted as consonant with his own ethics and with the true spirit of the Enlightenment, with the political clericalism then growing in Germany. Against clericalism he brought the accusation that those who were fighting Enlightenment were themselves trying to bring about the (perverse) end of the world. It was only two months later that the Berlin ministry replied, issuing its edict forbidding Kant to lecture or write on religious subjects.

In 1795 Kant published *Perpetual Peace, A Philosophical Sketch*. He had already dealt with the role of war in history, and other writers, e.g., William Penn, l'Abbé de St. Pierre, and Rousseau, had drawn plans for achieving world peace. But Kant saw the problem in a broader context than these men, and did not underestimate its difficulty as they had: like Hobbes, he saw the state of nature enduring in the sphere of international relations long after men had transcended it in their civil relations; he accordingly saw a comity of nations and a world commonwealth as the natural though difficult continuation of the historical processes he had already traced from barbarism to civil society. In this work all the strands of Kant's philosophy of morals, politics, and history are woven together

[3] In a letter to Biester, April 10, 1794; *Akademie* edn. of Kant's works (Berlin, 1902-38), XI, 477.

into a doctrine according to which republican government [4] and an enlightened citizenry are the mutually implicative conditions for lasting peace. Peace is a moral obligation; it must, therefore, be attainable. The study of history shows the gradual advance of mankind from barbarism to nationhood, and gives the directions needed for its further advance to cosmopolitanism and lasting peace.

The last essay in our volume, "The Old Question Raised Again: Is the Human Race Constantly Progressing?" was written when Kant was seventy-four years old and complaining even more than usual of the shortness of life and the magnitude of his unfinished tasks. The royal prohibition was still in force, and all his works had to be submitted to the censor in Berlin. There was some mismanagement in the Berlin office of Biester, to whom Kant had sent the manuscript, and Frederick William II died after the permit to print had been given but before Kant had been notified of the imprimatur. The delay in publication made Kant so impatient that he offered the manuscript to two other publishers, saying that he was not in the habit of working for nothing and throwing away what he had done. It was finally published in Königsberg in 1798 as the second part of a volume containing three independent essays written at various times on various subjects, under the general and not entirely appropriate title *The Strife of the Faculties*.[5]

---

4 Earlier, e.g., in "What is Enlightenment?" Kant had been sympathetic to the doctrine of enlightened despotism. But with the death of Frederick the Great, the accession of the unenlightened monarch Frederick William II, and the success (as he saw it) of the French Revolution, he moved closer to republicanism while still admitting the feasibility of constitutional monarchy; even at the end of his life he still thinks of civil reform as having little hope unless it comes from above. Cf. below, p. 152.

5 The German university of the eighteenth century was divided into four faculties, the three so-called higher faculties (theology, law, and medicine) and the lower, or philosophical, faculty. Kant was engaged in defending the rights of his faculty against the pretensions of the higher faculties; the higher faculties were organs of the state, charged with specific responsibilities in the education of clergymen, lawyers, and physicians, while the lower faculty was concerned only with liberal education. Hence

This essay is a self-contained work and owes its presence in
that book only to the accidents I have mentioned. The measured optimism of the old and enfeebled man, in this last piece
of writing which he undertook and brought to completion, is
shown here in his esteem for the French Revolution which
remained constant even when most of the earlier partisans of
it in Germany had fallen away and left him almost the last
and certainly the greatest of the "Jacobins" in Germany.[6]

III

The eighteenth century, the Age of Enlightenment or the
Age of Reason, is often thought of as lacking a "historical
sense." Modern scholarship does not entirely confirm this negative judgment. Not only was it an age of a few great historians,
e.g., Voltaire and Gibbon; it was the age of many philosophers
of history. The very name "philosophy of history" first appeared in this century, in the writings of Voltaire.

Philosophy of history in the modern sense—which is quite
different from that of Voltaire, who meant by it "history as
written by a *philosophe*"—has two problems, which we may
distinguish as the analytical and the synthetical. By the analyt-

---

the state, which might dictate the teaching in the higher faculties since
they were producing servants for the state, should not dictate to the lower
faculty, which was concerned with the education of men, not civil servants.
Nor should the higher faculties try to dictate to the lower faculty what
it should and should not teach. Kant's *Strife of the Faculties* is a defense
of *libertas philosophandi* and academic freedom. The first essay, "The
Strife of the Philosophical with the Theological Faculty" claims the right
of the former faculty to free inquiry into theological matters. The titles
of the second and third essays indicate that they will deal with conflicts
between the philosophical and the juristic and medical faculties, respectively. But they hardly do so at all; the reader of the second essay, translated in this volume, will see how little it has to do with this academic
matter; and the third essay, "On the Power of the Mind through Mere
Resolution to Master its Sickly Feelings," has just as little.

[6] G. P. Gooch, *Germany and the French Revolution* (London, 1920)
illustrates Kant's repute as a Jacobin: there was a rumor that Kant had
accepted an invitation from Sieyès to come to Paris as his adviser!

ical philosophy of history, I refer to the epistemology of historiography. The eighteenth century did not, it is true, make much progress in this field because it did not clearly see the difficulty of the problems to which this discipline applies. History was, if I may say so, practiced from a philosophically naive point of view. Pierre Bayle and Hume were, to be sure, sophisticated in their understanding of the general problems of historical evidence; Herder criticized the abstract reasoning of the *philosophes* when applied to history and called for a more intuitive method; and Kant rigorously and explicitly considered "regulative Ideas" [7] for historical synthesis in their relation to evidence. But the problems of relativism, historicism, and *Wertfreiheit* [freedom from value judgment] belong to a later time, though when they were raised in their full complexity it was by German philosophers imbued with the spirit of Kantianism: Dilthey, Simmel, Windelband, Troeltsch, Rickert, Weber.[8] They tried to do for the study of history what Kant had done for the study of nature, viz., to discover its a priori presuppositions and limits. But their analytical problems were not those of Kant's century.

The synthetic task of the philosophy of history is to find the meaning of history, the significance of the whole sweep of the past in man's conception of himself and of his place in the world and in time. The eighteenth century was luxuriant in the growth of philosophies of history in this synthetic or speculative sense. They ranged from that of Bossuet, written at the end of the preceding century in the light of the Sun King, showing the guiding hand of Providence in all human affairs, to that of Condorcet, written at the end of the eighteenth century in the shadow of the guillotine, representing human resourcefulness as the motor of inexorable progress. Between these two dates and intellectual zones, there arose the intermediate syntheses by Rousseau, Voltaire, Diderot, d'Alembert, Turgot, Montesquieu, Burke, Mendelssohn, Lessing, and Her-

---

[7] For the Kantian sense of "Idea," see below, p. xix and note 15.

[8] Cf. Carlo Antoni, *From History to Sociology* (trans. H. V. White; Detroit, 1959), who traces this development.

der.[9] All of these men were studied by Kant, and we have seen that it was the writing of Herder which gave him the occasion for some of his own ventures into the philosophy of history.

Most of these philosophers of history were concerned with a small number of central questions, and, in spite of wide variation in detail and some few mavericks like Burke and Rousseau, they gave a set of more or less common answers to them; these answers constituted a central part of the ideology of the Age of Reason. Let us consider the central questions and indicate the typical answers, remembering always, of course, that a "typical answer" is a kind of average of many more or less different answers.

(1) *What is the status of the present age when compared to the past?* Earlier thinkers had seen the Golden Age as lying in the past, and history as a decline from it; in the preceding century there had been the famous and pervasive "quarrel of the ancients and the moderns," [10] and by the eighteenth century the partisans of the moderns had won. Gibbon, to be sure, saw history as the "triumph of religion and barbarism," and Rousseau saw it as the story of the enchainment of man who was born free; but most of the writers were clearly and enthusiastically if naively on the side of "progress" and especially of the progress that had been made, they thought, since the end of the medieval period.

(2) *How is this progress discerned and measured?* The clearest criterion was the advance in knowledge; some went further and held that there had been a like advance in literary and artistic excellence; but gradually the eudaemonistic criterion

---

[9] Gian-battista Vico's works do not fall in this main tradition, and they did not have any influence on the Enlightenment philosophy of history until Herder, through Montesquieu, learned from them.

[10] The dispute concerning the relative merits of ancient and modern literature (and, by extension, ancient and modern science), which was waged primarily in France (Fontenelle, *Digression sur les anciens et les modernes* [1688]; Perrault, *Parallèles des anciens et des modernes* [1688-97]; and Boileau, *Réflexions sur Longin* [1693]) and was best known in England through Swift's *The Battle of the Books* (1697). On the quarrel in science, cf. R. F. Jones, *Ancients and Moderns* (St. Louis, 1961).

replaced or summed up all the others. Men are now happier than their forefathers had been. Happiness is the purpose of life, and the eighteenth century is the happiest of centuries; but our posterity will be even happier than we.

(3) *What made this progress possible?* In the Age of Reason, the *philosophes* gave only one answer: the use of reason, as taught by Descartes, Bacon, Locke, and Leibniz, unfettered by superstition and tradition, devoted to conquering nature for human use and to improving human institutions.

(4) *What are its future prospects?* In answering this question, the optimism [11] of the century is most obvious: given time—and it often seemed that only a few generations were needed—a new golden age could be brought into being. The French (and, to a lesser extent, the American) Revolution was a sign to many—even to Condorcet who would die in it—of the dawn of a new day; Wordsworth, looking back upon it, could say, "Bliss was it in that dawn to be alive/But to be young was very heaven."

(5) *What, then, shall we do?* Accumulate knowledge; spread it freely among men; give them, or help them establish, governments which will permit them to use this knowledge for their own betterment; establish a league of nations to prevent wars. As the beginning, Voltaire's *Écrasons l'infâme!*; as the next step, Kant's *Sapere aude!* "Have courage to use your own reason." [12]

Kant's mature interpretation of history is his application of the principal theses of his critical philosophy to these widespread beliefs of his time. None of them he originated; most of them he accepted when young and modified when old; all of them he illuminated.

[11] The reader must not forget that we are here, as throughout this section, speaking of "typical answers." That the belief in progress was not as universal and jejune as it has since appeared, and that it had, even in the Enlightenment, to struggle against belief in flux and decadence is shown in detail by Henry Vyvenberg, *Historical Pessimism in the French Enlightenment* (Cambridge, Mass., 1958).

[12] Voltaire, Letter to d'Alembert of June 23, 1760; Kant, see below, p. 3.

IV

There are three teachings in Kant's critical philosophy which must be clearly understood if we are to see the problem of history as he saw it. These teachings, two of them on the surface anti-historical, are: (1) causal mechanism, (2) the primacy of pure practical reason, and (3) the regulative principle of teleology.

(1) The *Critique of Pure Reason* and the *Prolegomena* teach that the world we know is a system of phenomena under laws, the principal law being that of necessary causal connection. We understand the world of phenomena because the mind gives laws to the appearances of the senses, converting the "rhapsody of sensations" into the orderly conception of a world of atoms, stars, sticks and stones, and human events. In this world, human actions are as predictable as eclipses of the sun and moon; nothing happens by chance; nothing happens for the sake of anything else; there is no providential hand of God visible in nature, neither in the evolution of planets nor in the affairs of men. Though we do not know enough to predict the time, place, and manner of many natural and human events, nonetheless they are all causally determined down to their last detail, and in the large they are in fact predictable.

(2) The *Critique of Practical Reason* and the *Foundations of the Metaphysics of Morals* teach that man is under absolute and irrefragable obligations. The moral law of his obligation comes from his own reason, not from nature and not from God. Man is the legislator of the moral law through his own pure practical reason. But what if practical reason commands him to do something under the moral law that it seems to his theoretical reason he cannot do under the causal law of nature? Kant replies: pure practical reason has the primacy over the speculative reason; in spite of appearances, man can do what he ought to do. He may not do so, but the fault lies in his weakness of will and evil disposition, not in nature's sway of

blind necessity. And what if it seems that the moral ideal cannot be achieved because of the weakness of will against the importunities of sense and the mechanism of nature? Kant replies: the world of nature, the only one we know, is a construction put upon appearances; it is not reality, which we do not and cannot know. Hence what is not possible in the world understood as nature may be possible in the world as it really is, and we must either declare the moral command nugatory or postulate the final attainability of the goals which the moral command places before us.

(3) The *Critique of Judgment* teaches the proper use of the concept of purpose. Purpose seems as alien to the physical world described by Kant as to that described by Lucretius. It has often, though wrongly, been said that for Kant not even moral acts can have a purpose; yet Kant sees the concept of purpose as essential for our practical reason, which is concerned with human projects and aspirations. To resolve the antinomy between natural determinism and freedom without surrendering either, Kant shows that in science, especially in biology, it is necessary to make use of the concept of purpose in the discovery of causes themselves. Whatever may be true in principle, we cannot in fact explain biological phenomena or find their mechanical causes without treating them as if they were products of a natural teleology; there will never be a "Newton of a blade of grass." Purpose is a necessary regulative Idea for the interpretation of nature; a fortiori we must use it in understanding human nature and history. And if our teleological interpretation of nature is to be systematic and unitary, there must be some final purpose in it—otherwise it would be a world of means without an end, as disorganized as a mechanical world would be if its physical laws, like Kepler's and Galileo's, were not reducible to Newton's. The final purpose of the world, that which is end and should not be merely means, Kant finds in man, rational man legislating and obeying moral law in an otherwise meaningless world. Granted this, the world itself must then be interpreted as the stage for moral

evolution and human action, not "a dull affair, soundless, scentless, colourless; merely the hurrying of material, endlessly, meaninglessly." [13]

These are the fixed points in the Kantian philosophy, developed in the years from 1781 to 1790, the period during which Kant began his work in the philosophy of history.

V

Now we are prepared to answer the question we raised at the end of Section One: What connection is there between Kant's theoretical and practical philosophy, on the one hand, and the philosophy of history on the other?

Philosophy, for Kant, is a priori knowledge from concepts; history is empirical, not a priori, knowledge of human events. Moral philosophy requires us to assume that man is a non-temporal *homo noumenon,* possessing real freedom; science deals with man only as a temporal *homo phaenomenon,* behaving under laws of nature. But human actions, including moral actions, take place on the stage of nature, and history is the recounting of the movement of man from the state of being a mere part of the mechanism of nature to the state of being the creator of and citizen in the world of culture, where he can eventually come to know and perform his duties and realize his moral ends.

The philosophy of history, then, like the philosophy of art and the philosophy of biology as expounded in the *Critique of Judgment,*[14] must be a conceptual link between Kant's two worlds of nature and morality. This was, I think, Kant's intention. I do not wish to minimize the influence of his intense

[13] A. N. Whitehead, *Science and the Modern World* (New York, 1925), p. 80. Kant's view of Nature in its relation to the final purpose is given in *Critique of Judgment,* §§ 83-84, these two sections being among Kant's most important discussions in the philosophy of history.

[14] Renato Composto (*La quarta critica kantiana;* Palermo, 1954) goes so far as to treat the collection of historical writings as constituting a fourth *Critique.*

interest in the facts of history and his enthusiasm for the progressive movements of his time, as if to suggest that his writings on history were inspired only by a technical need in the architectonic of his critical philosophy. Nor do I suggest that he worked out the philosophy of history in the painstaking and minute detail that marked his theory of aesthetic and teleological judgment. What we have here is hardly more than a series of sketches, with repeated reminders that the full elaboration of a history according to Kantian principles is a job for some future historian, not for Kant himself. But I do believe that these relations among the *Critiques* give us the clue to Kant's turning to the philosophy of history at the same time that he was moving toward the construction of his critical ethics of pure practical reason and examining its relation to the science of nature.

The unwary reader, oblivious of this connection, may not at first realize how much is implied and presupposed in the very title, "Idea for a Universal History." It is easy to see, of course, that Kant is projecting an "idea" or proposal that some future historian might take up and develop into a real universal history of mankind, in the manner of Herder. But what may not be so obvious is that the word "Idea" has a precise technical meaning in Kant's philosophy, and that this essay is the presentation of an Idea in that strict sense.[15]

Kant takes the word "Idea" from Plato,[16] though he does not ascribe metaphysical reality and power to Ideas, as Plato often did. An Idea for Kant is like Plato's Idea, however, in being a conception for which no experience can give us an exemplar, yet a conception which is not arbitrarily constructed by the imagination. But whereas Plato thought the Ideas were objects of pure reason in a noumenal world in which the world of sense participates by imitating the Ideas, Kant thought of

[15] When the word is used in the technical sense, as a translation of the German word *Idee*, it is appropriate to capitalize it, to distinguish it from the more ordinary use of the word, e.g., "I have little idea of life in the Stone Age"—which, in German, is usually *Vorstellung*.
[16] Cf. *Critique of Pure Reason*, A 313ff. = B 370ff.; see below, p. 150.

them as necessary creations of the human mind with no known metaphysical existence. Necessary, though, for what? Kant believed that they were necessary for the guidance of our theoretical knowledge and practical or moral experience, holding before us an unrealized systematic goal for our piecemeal dealings with particular problems.

Ideas may be either theoretical or practical. The teleological organization of nature is a theoretical Idea; it regulates our inquiry and leads us to discover causes, even though an explanation in terms of purpose serves only until the mechanical causes are discovered—whereupon the teleological explanation of this thing is replaced by the mechanical, and the teleological Idea remains only to guide us in making the next step.

Practical Ideas are conceptions of moral goals and perfections which we should strive to reach through our own actions. They are archetypes; Plato's *Republic* obviously presents an Idea in this sense, as Kant points out. The Idea of a perfect commonwealth cannot be learned from history, for the ideal state never existed and may never exist on earth; but "In heaven there is laid up a pattern [or Idea] of it, which he who desires may behold, and, beholding, may set his own house in order." [17] Virtue is another such Idea; Kant says that no clear and indubitable example of virtue can be found in all history,[18] but the Idea of virtue, created by human reason, is the standard for judging all imperfect human deeds and the archetype which we ought to embody in our characters.

The word "Idea" in the title of the essay has these meanings. It is not a mere synonym for "consideration" or "view" or "sketch" or the like. It tells us that Kant is here to present a model or plan or Platonic Idea of history. It is an Idea partially manifested in the actual historical process; it can be beheld by the historian, who will then write history in accord-

[17] *Republic,* end of Book IX. Kant, of course, does not think of it as existing anywhere.

[18] *Foundations of the Metaphysics of Morals,* "Library of Liberal Arts," No. 113 (New York, 1959), p. 23.

ance with it and thereby help mankind along the hard road to the fuller realization of it.

Though Kant uses the word "Idea" in the singular in the title of his paper, there are actually three fundamental Ideas in all his historical writings: Nature, as a theoretical Idea, and the State and a League of Nations, as practical ideas. We must examine each.

VI

Nature as an Idea is not just the machine of eighteenth-century physics and astronomy. Astronomy and physics give its anatomy, as it were, but Nature is an organic whole each part of which is necessary to the others, so that a comprehension of the whole is essential to the correct understanding of any part.[19] This is Nature as understood by the Stoics, not the Epicureans; the Nature of Shaftesbury and Pope, not of Holbach and La Mettrie; the Nature of Spinoza or Leibniz, not "a damp place, with birds."

In the *Critique of Pure Reason* Kant analyzed the presuppositions of the Newtonian conception of nature, and in his *Universal Natural History and Theory of the Heavens* (1755) he had gone even farther than Newton did toward making it possible for Laplace later to say to Napoleon that astronomers had no need for the hypothesis of God. For Newton had supposed that God created the solar system as we know it, and that He occasionally intervened in the universe, but Kant attempted to explain even the origin of the solar system using only the principles of Newton's mechanics. The world-machine

[19] "All are but parts of one stupendous whole
Whose body Nature is, and God the soul.
. . . .
All nature is but art, unknown to thee;
All chance, direction thou canst not see;
All discord, harmony not understood;
All partial evil, universal good."
(Pope, *Essay on Man*, I, lines 267-68, 289-93)

is one Idea; but in the *Critique of Judgment* Kant put beside
it this older conception of Nature which can function in
science as a regulative Idea, aiding in the discovery of mechanical causes.

In the philosophy of history, after acknowledging causal determinism,[20] it is this more ancient conception of Nature as
the womb of history that takes the place of Providence [21] or
reason as the mainspring of human progress. Thus the story
of man's fall is interpreted in a purely naturalistic way, and
the origin of man's culture is explained without recourse to
revelation or to noble savages in committee drawing up a social
contract. Nature is mankind's mother (or, rather, stepmother,
as Kant sometimes wryly suggests); [22] she has not made it easy
for man to progress from barbarism and she has been neglectful
of the individual, caring only for the species and providing
no equitable distribution of her favors. By sowing discord
among men and endowing them with an "unsocial sociability,"
she has made it both possible and necessary for them to make
their own way. Man owes her nothing but his existence, for
Nature willed it that "he should partake of no other happiness
or perfection than that which he himself, independently of
[natural] instinct, has created by his own reason." [23]

The second Idea is that of the state or civil society. The teleological Idea of Nature involves the notion that Nature does
nothing in vain, and that it is Nature's plan that what she has
created shall reach its full and perfect development. Reason
was not given to man by Nature in order to make him happy;
we know this, because we know that reason is ill suited to this
purpose and, had this been Nature's purpose, she would have

[20] See below, p. 11.

[21] See below, p. 13.

[22] *Critique of Practical Reason*, "Library of Liberal Arts," No. 52 (New
York, 1956), p. 152.

[23] See below, p. 13. Rousseau, of course, denied a natural unsocial sociability, and held that "private hostility between man and man cannot
obtain either in a state of nature where there is no generally accepted
system of private property, or in a state of society where law is the supreme authority" (*Social Contract*, chap. 4).

endowed man only with instincts adequate to it.[24] Since Nature does nothing in vain, we must find the purpose for which reason is perfectly and uniquely adequate, and this is the creation of culture (and, eventually, of morality). Thus Kant rejected the eudaemonistic criterion of progress and replaced it with a criterion of the degree to which reason is developed and exercised as an instrument of culture and source of morality. Now culture is not only the fruit of reason; it is also a condition for the perfect growth and full employment of reason itself. Hence Nature wills that man shall accomplish for himself something she cannot provide for him: culture, and life under reasonable laws. This, then, is the assignment Nature gives to her sons: "the achievement of a universal civic society which administers law among men." [25] For the solution of this problem, Nature, not morality and not divine revelation, provides the tool; it is the human instinct of unsocial sociability combined with intelligence. This is a task that does not require that man be by nature good, as Rousseau believed; it is a problem that can be solved "even for a race of devils, if only they are intelligent." [26]

This in itself, however, creates an entirely new set of problems, because man is a beast and needs a master, but the master is no less a beast.[27] The ruler, to control his subjects, tries to stop the free exercise of reason, which, though it is not possible without a strong government, is a threat to those rulers without strong armies and stable institutions. Strong government, therefore, is both a condition of and a hazard to Enlightenment; if government oversteps its bounds, especially in matters of religion, it becomes the earthly representative of Antichrist.[28] With progress in Enlightenment, however, there is a gain in self-government (republicanism) which increases the scope of intelligent and responsible freedom without diminish-

[24] *Foundations of the Metaphysics of Morals*, p. 12.
[25] See below, p. 16.
[26] See below, p. 112; for Rousseau's view, cf. *Social Contract*, chap. 6, end.
[27] See below, pp. 17, 50.
[28] See below, p. 84.

ing the stability of just society. Frederick the Great is seen as
the enlightened despot who, because of his strong army, could
afford to let his subjects "argue as much as they will" so long
as they obeyed. The Age of Enlightenment is accordingly
called by Kant "the century of Frederick." [29] Later he saw the
progress of Enlightenment and self-government confirmed in
the world-wide response to the French Revolution and its
motto of liberty and equality.[30]

The achievement of republican government (which is compatible with an hereditary monarchy, if the monarchy is con-
stitutionally limited) with an enlightened citizenry freely practicing its religions and pursuing knowledge, however, is
involved also in the solution of another problem which, in our
own day, seems much more difficult. It is to Kant's credit that
he saw, better than sentimental Utopians, the intimate connection between the two problems. The other problem is the
establishment of a commonwealth of nations for the maintenance of peace. Kant saw that war is "the continuation of [dy-
nastic] politics by other means," and that it is often undertaken for trivial purposes—sometimes domestic purposes—which
are in conflict with the rights of man. Let men rule themselves,
however, and then their rights—which are entirely different
from the interests of princes—will prevail and no longer be
jeopardized by irresponsible war-making. But an alliance, even
with despots (such as Kant thought he saw in the Peace of
Basel between the King of Prussia and the revolutionary government of France) would give opportunity for the spread of
Enlightenment (e.g., by cutting down on war expenses and permitting more money to be spent on education) and the gradual
reform of government itself.[31] Since the first task, the establishment of a civil society, cannot be permanently solved on a

[29] See below, p. 9.
[30] See below, p. 143. But he had little use for the sentiment of frater-
nity; cf. his "Concerning the Common Saying: That may be true in theory
but does not apply to practice" (1793), in *The Philosophy of Kant*, trans.
C. J. Friedrich (New York, 1949), p. 416.
[31] See below, p. 152.

local or piecemeal basis, Nature, having used war as one of her means for spreading mankind over the earth and bringing them together in large societies, thereby "guarantees" [32] the cessation of war as an end which man has a duty to achieve. But does this mean that Nature, in thus promising, at some indefinite time in the future, the ultimate success of one of mankind's morally obligatory projects, makes men moral? No, this is beyond Nature's competence. Nature is the stage for civilization and culture, a "simulacrum of morality" in a system of external law. Without this, there can be no morality; but without morality, even culture is but "glittering misery" and "bustling folly." [33] There is implanted in man by Nature a disposition to morality, but there is no natural morality. Morality is the work of freedom, a free creation of pure practical reason. It cannot be comprehended empirically by history or theoretically by philosophy; philosophy teaches us to comprehend only its incomprehensibility.[34]

The philosophy of history, therefore, is not a history of morals but a history of man's coming of age, to the point where he becomes moral by the free exercise of his rational will; and it is a preview of the future, showing how "the destiny of the race can be fulfilled here on earth." [35] With freedom, which transcends the historical and natural order, we enter the realm of faith and action.

"How is history a priori possible?" asks Kant, in a question reminiscent of the question of his *Critiques*. He wittily answers: it is possible if "the diviner [i.e., the historian of events which have not yet happened] himself creates and contrives the events which he announces in advance." [36] That is, the Idea of history will be realized only if we act in the faith that it can be realized, and produce those events which will exemplify it.

32 See below, p. 106.
33 See below, pp. 21, 140.
34 *Foundations of the Metaphysics of Morals*, p. 83.
35 See below, p. 25.
36 See below, p. 137.

The establishment of a genuine moral commonwealth (not just a civil society under external law) has, as its necessary condition, the progress recounted in past history; but its sufficient condition is "a kind of new creation (supernatural influence)" [37] in which moral law comes to be regarded as if it were a divine, not a human, ordinance. History has brought us to the present; there are indications, Kant thinks, that the progress will continue; but that it will continue is predicated upon our own faith in the autarchy of will [38] and free acts, not on settled empirical knowledge of the past extended inductively to the future. The movement of history or the trend of the times does not, therefore, exempt men from their moral responsibility for seeking the reign of law over the whole world. The future will be the work of men, not a conclusion waiting to be drawn from premises already discovered by historians. Each moral act at the time it is done is, as it were, an absolutely new beginning, not determined by history or by Nature. History brings us to each present; but in each future we are on our own.[39]

LEWIS WHITE BECK

[37] See below, p. 151. Cf. also *Religion within the Limits of Reason Alone* (New York, 1960), pp. 36, 90-92 on the moral commonwealth and the moral act "as if it had no past."

[38] Cf. *Fortschritte der Metaphysik (Akademie* edn.), XX, 295; L. W. Beck, *Commentary on Kant's Critique of Practical Reason* (Chicago, 1960), p. 208.

[39] The editor is grateful to Professor Willson H. Coates for instructive discussions of the content of this Introduction.

SKETCH OF KANT'S LIFE AND WORK

Immanuel Kant was born in Königsberg, East Prussia, on April 22, 1724. His family were Pietists, a Protestant sect somewhat like the Quakers and early Methodists. Pietism's deeply ethical orientation and singular lack of emphasis upon theological dogmatism became a part of Kant's character and a determining factor in his philosophy. After attending the University of Königsberg and serving as tutor in several aristocratic families, Kant became a lecturer in the University. He held this position for fifteen years, lecturing and writing on metaphysics, logic, ethics, geography, anthropology, mathematics, and the natural sciences. In the sciences he made significant but, at the time, little-recognized contributions, especially in physics, astronomy, geology, and meteorology.

In 1770 he was appointed Professor of Logic and Metaphysics in Königsberg, and in 1781 he published his most important work, the *Critique of Pure Reason*. This work opened up new fields of study and problems for him at an age when most men are ready to retire; but for Kant there followed a period of nearly twenty years of unremitting labor and unparalleled accomplishment. Merely a list of the most important writings shows this: *Prolegomena to Any Future Metaphysics* (1783); *Idea for a Universal History* (1784); *What is Enlightenment?* (1784); *Foundations of the Metaphysics of Morals* (1785); *Metaphysical Foundations of Natural Science* (1786); *Conjectural Beginning of Human History* (1786); revised edition of *Critique of Pure Reason* (1787); *Critique of Practical Reason* (1788); *Critique of Judgment* (1790); *Religion within the Limits of Reason Alone* (1793); *The End of All Things* (1794); *Perpetual Peace* (1795); *Metaphysics of Ethics* (1797); *The Strife of the Faculties* (1798); and *Anthropology from a Pragmatic Point of View* (1798). During all of this time Kant was carrying a heavy load of academic duties, and during part of it he was restricted in his writing and lecturing because of the government's prohibition on his dealing with religious questions. He died in Königsberg, February 12, 1804.

Kant's personality, or at least a caricature of it, is well known. Most people who know nothing else of Kant do believe that the housewives of Königsberg used to set their clocks by the regular afternoon walk he took. His life was said to pass like the most regular of regular verbs. But a truer picture of his personality—less pedantic, Prussian, and Puritanical—comes to us from Johann Gottfried Herder: [1]

> I have had the good fortune to know a philosopher. He was my teacher. In his prime he had the happy sprightliness of youth; he continued to have it, I believe, even as a very old man. His broad forehead, built for thought, was the seat of an imperturable cheerfulness and joy. Speech, the richest in thought, flowed from his lips. Playfulness, wit, and humor were at his command. His lectures were the most entertaining talks. His mind, which examined Leibniz, Wolff, Baumgarten, Crusius, and Hume, and investigated the laws of nature of Newton, Kepler, and the physicists, comprehended equally the newest works of Rousseau . . . and the latest discoveries in science. He weighed them all, and always came back to the unbiased knowledge of nature and to the moral worth of man. The history of men and peoples, natural history and science, mathematics and observation, were the sources from which he enlivened his lectures and conversation. No cabal, no sect, no prejudice, no desire for fame, could ever tempt him in the slightest away from broadening and illuminating the truth. He incited and gently forced others to think for themselves; despotism was foreign to his mind. This man, whom I name with the greatest gratitude and respect, was Immanuel Kant.

L. W. B.

[1] *Briefe zur Beförderung der Humanität*, in *Sämmtliche Werke*, ed. Suphan (Berlin, 1877-1913), XVIII, 324-25.

SELECTED BIBLIOGRAPHY

GENERAL WORKS ON KANT

Copleston, Frederick. *A History of Philosophy*. Vol. VI, *From Wolff to Kant*. London, 1960.

Körner, S. *Kant*. London, 1955.

Lindsay, A. D. *Kant*. London, 1934.

Paulsen, Friedrich. *Immanuel Kant, His Life and Doctrine*. New York, 1902.

WORKS RELATING TO KANT'S PHILOSOPHY OF HISTORY

Armstrong, A. C. "Kant's Philosophy of Peace and War," *Journal of Philosophy*, XXVIII (1931), 197-204.

Axinn, Sidney. "Kant, Logic, and the Concept of Mankind," *Ethics*, XLVIII (1958), 286-91.

————. *A Study of Kant's Philosophy of History*. (Dissertation, University of Pennsylvania, 1955). Ann Arbor, 1955.

Barth, Karl. *Protestant Thought from Rousseau to Ritschl*. Esp. Chaps. I-IV. New York, 1959.

Beck, L. W. Translator's Introduction to Kant, *Perpetual Peace*. "Library of Liberal Arts," No. 54. New York, 1957.

Becker, Carl L. *The Heavenly City of the Eighteenth Century Philosophers*. New Haven, 1932.

Bourke, John. "Kant's Doctrine of 'Perpetual Peace,'" *Philosophy*, XVII (1942), 324-33.

Bury, John. *The Idea of Progress*. New York, 1932, 1955.

Cassirer, Ernst. *The Philosophy of the Enlightenment*. Ch. V. Boston, 1951.

Clark, Robert T., Jr. *Herder, His Life and Thought*. Berkeley, 1955.

Collingwood, R. G. *The Idea of History*. Oxford, 1946.

Composto, R. *La quarta critica kantiana*. Palermo, 1954.

Fackenheim, Emil L. "Kant's Concept of History," *Kant-Studien*, XLVIII (1957), 381-98.

————. "Kant and Radical Evil," *University of Toronto Quarterly*, XXIII (1954), 339-53.

Flint, Robert. *The Philosophy of History in France and Germany.* Book II, Chaps. IV, V. London, 1874.

Friedrich, Carl Joachim. *Inevitable Peace.* Cambridge, Mass., 1948.

Hancock, Roger N. "Ethics and History in Kant and Mill," *Ethics,* LXVIII (1957), 56-60.

Hibben, J. G. *The Philosophy of the Enlightenment.* New York, 1910.

Medicus, F. "Kants Philosophie der Geschichte," *Kant-Studien,* VII (1902), 1-23, 171-229.

Menzer, P. *Kants Lehre von der Entwicklung in Natur und Geschichte.* Berlin, 1911.

Reiss, H. S. "Kant and the Right of Rebellion," *Journal of the History of Ideas,* XVII (1956), 179-92.

Ruyssen, Théodore. "La philosophie de l'histoire selon Kant," *Annales de philosophie politique,* IV (1962), 33-51.

Schrecker, Paul. "Kant et la révolution Française," *Revue philosophique,* XXVIII (1939), 394-425.

Schwarz, Wolfgang. "Kant's Philosophy of Law and International Peace," *Philosophy and Phenomenological Research,* XXIII (1962), 71-80.

Walsh, W. H. *An Introduction to the Philosophy of History.* London, 1951.

Wells, G. A. *Herder and After.* The Hague, 1959.

NOTE ON THE TEXT

All the translations in this volume follow the text of the seventh and eighth volumes of the edition by the *Königliche Preussische Akademie der Wissenschaften* (Berlin, 1902-38). Marginal numbers refer to pages in that standard edition.

The translations of *Perpetual Peace* and "What is Enlightenment?" are reprinted from the editions of the "Library of Liberal Arts," Numbers 54 and 113 respectively. The translations of "Idea for a Universal History" by Mr. Beck, of "Conjectural Beginning of Human History" by Mr. Fackenheim, and of the Reviews of Herder, "The End of All Things," and "An Old Question Raised Again" by Mr. Anchor, have not previously been published.

Notes and other material supplied by the editor or translator are in square brackets.

KANT ON HISTORY

WHAT IS ENLIGHTENMENT?

Enlightenment is man's release from his self-incurred tutelage. Tutelage is man's inability to make use of his understanding without direction from another. Self-incurred is this tutelage when its cause lies not in lack of reason but in lack of
resolution and courage to use it without direction from another. *Sapere aude!* [1] "Have courage to use your own reason!"
—that is the motto of enlightenment.

Laziness and cowardice are the reasons why so great a portion of mankind, after nature has long since discharged them
from external direction (*naturaliter maiorennes*), nevertheless
remains under lifelong tutelage, and why it is so easy for others
to set themselves up as their guardians. It is so easy not to be
of age. If I have a book which understands for me, a pastor
who has a conscience for me, a physician who decides my diet,
and so forth, I need not trouble myself. I need not think, if I
can only pay—others will readily undertake the irksome work
for me.

That the step to competence is held to be very dangerous by
the far greater portion of mankind (and by the entire fair sex)
—quite apart from its being arduous—is seen to by those
guardians who have so kindly assumed superintendence over
them. After the guardians have first made their domestic cattle
dumb and have made sure that these placid creatures will not
dare take a single step without the harness of the cart to which
they are tethered, the guardians then show them the danger
which threatens if they try to go alone. Actually, however, this
danger is not so great, for by falling a few times they would
finally learn to walk alone. But an example of this failure

1 ["Dare to know!" (Horace, *Ars poetica*). This was the motto adopted
in 1736 by the Society of the Friends of Truth, an important circle in the
German Enlightenment.]

makes them timid and ordinarily frightens them away from all further trials.

For any single individual to work himself out of the life under tutelage which has become almost his nature is very difficult. He has come to be fond of this state, and he is for the present really incapable of making use of his reason, for no one has ever let him try it out. Statutes and formulas, those mechanical tools of the rational employment or rather mis-employment of his natural gifts, are the fetters of an everlast-ing tutelage. Whoever throws them off makes only an uncer-tain leap over the narrowest ditch because he is not accustomed to that kind of free motion. Therefore, there are few who have succeeded by their own exercise of mind both in freeing them-selves from incompetence and in achieving a steady pace.

But that the public should enlighten itself is more possible; indeed, if only freedom is granted, enlightenment is almost sure to follow. For there will always be some independent thinkers, even among the established guardians of the great masses, who, after throwing off the yoke of tutelage from their own shoulders, will disseminate the spirit of the rational ap-preciation of both their own worth and every man's vocation for thinking for himself. But be it noted that the public, which has first been brought under this yoke by their guardians, forces the guardians themselves to remain bound when it is incited to do so by some of the guardians who are themselves capable of some enlightenment—so harmful is it to implant prejudices, for they later take vengeance on their cultivators or on their descendants. Thus the public can only slowly attain enlightenment. Perhaps a fall of personal despotism or of avaricious or tyrannical oppression may be accomplished by revolution, but never a true reform in ways of thinking. Rather, new prejudices will serve as well as old ones to harness the great unthinking masses.

For this enlightenment, however, nothing is required but freedom, and indeed the most harmless among all the things to which this term can properly be applied. It is the freedom to make public use of one's reason at every point.[2] But I hear on all sides, "Do not argue!" The officer says: "Do not argue but drill!" The tax collector: "Do not argue but pay!" The cleric: "Do not argue but believe!" Only one prince in the world says, "Argue as much as you will, and about what you will, but obey!" Everywhere there is restriction on freedom.

Which restriction is an obstacle to enlightenment, and which is not an obstacle but a promoter of it? I answer: The public use of one's reason must always be free, and it alone can bring about enlightenment among men. The private use of reason, on the other hand, may often be very narrowly restricted without particularly hindering the progress of enlightenment. By the public use of one's reason I understand the use which a person makes of it as a scholar before the reading public. Private use I call that which one may make of it in a particular civil post or office which is entrusted to him. Many affairs which are conducted in the interest of the community require a certain mechanism through which some members of the community must passively conduct themselves with an artificial unanimity, so that the government may direct them to public ends, or at least prevent them from destroying those ends. Here argument is certainly not allowed—one must obey. But so far as a part of the mechanism regards himself at the same time as a member of the whole community or of a society of world citizens, and thus in the role of a scholar who addresses the public (in the proper sense of the word) through his writings, he certainly can argue without hurting the affairs for which he is in part responsible as a passive member. Thus it would be ruinous for an officer in service to debate about the suitability or utility of a command given to him by his superior; he must obey. But the right to make remarks on errors in the military service and to lay them before the public for judgment cannot equitably be refused him as a scholar. The citizen cannot refuse to pay the taxes imposed on him; indeed,

[2] [It is this freedom Kant claimed later in his conflict with the censor, deferring to the censor in the "private" use of reason, i.e., in his lectures.]

an impudent complaint at those levied on him can be punished as a scandal (as it could occasion general refractoriness). But the same person nevertheless does not act contrary to his duty as a citizen when, as a scholar, he publicly expresses **38** his thoughts on the inappropriateness or even the injustice of these levies. Similarly a clergyman is obligated to make his sermon to his pupils in catechism and his congregation conform to the symbol of the church which he serves, for he has been accepted on his condition. But as a scholar he has complete freedom, even the calling, to communicate to the public all his carefully tested and well-meaning thoughts on that which is erroneous in the symbol and to make suggestions for the better organization of the religious body and church. In doing this there is nothing that could be laid as a burden on his conscience. For what he teaches as a consequence of his office as a representative of the church, this he considers something about which he has no freedom to teach according to his own lights; it is something which he is appointed to propound at the dictation of and in the name of another. He will say, "Our church teaches this or that; those are the proofs which it adduces." He thus extracts all practical uses for his congregation from statutes to which he himself would not subscribe with full conviction but to the enunciation of which he can very well pledge himself because it is not impossible that truth lies hidden in them, and, in any case, there is at least nothing in them contradictory to inner religion. For if he believed he had found such in them, he could not conscientiously discharge the duties of his office; he would have to give it up. The use, therefore, which an appointed teacher makes of his reason before his congregation is merely private, because this congregation is only a domestic one (even if it be a large gathering); with respect to it, as a priest, he is not free, nor can he be free, because he carries out the orders of another. But as a scholar, whose writings speak to his public, the world, the clergyman in the public use of his reason enjoys an unlimited freedom to use his own reason and to speak in his own person. That the guardians of the people (in spiritual things) should themselves be incompetent is an absurdity which amounts to the eternalization of absurdities.

But would not a society of clergymen, perhaps a church conference or a venerable classis (as they call themselves among the Dutch), be justified in obligating itself by oath to a certain unchangeable symbol in order to enjoy an unceasing guardianship over each of its members and thereby over the people as a whole, and even to make it eternal? I answer that this is altogether impossible. Such a contract, made to shut off all further enlightenment from the human race, is absolutely null and void even if confirmed by the supreme power, by parliaments, and by the most ceremonious of peace treaties. An age cannot bind itself and ordain to put the succeeding one into such a condition that it cannot extend its (at best very occasional) knowledge, purify itself of errors, and progress in general enlightenment. That would be a crime against human nature, the proper destination of which lies precisely in this progress; and the descendants would be fully justified in rejecting those decrees as having been made in an unwarranted and malicious manner.

The touchstone of everything that can be concluded as a law for a people lies in the question whether the people could have imposed such a law on itself. Now such a religious compact might be possible for a short and definitely limited time, as it were, in expectation of a better. One might let every citizen, and especially the clergyman, in the role of scholar, make his comments freely and publicly, i.e., through writing, on the erroneous aspects of the present institution. The newly introduced order might last until insight into the nature of these things had become so general and widely approved that through uniting their voices (even if not unanimously) they could bring a proposal to the throne to take those congregations under protection which had united into a changed religious organization according to their better ideas, without, however, hindering others who wish to remain in the order. But to unite in a permanent religious institution which is not to be subject to doubt before the public even in the lifetime of one man, and thereby to make a period of time fruitless in the progress of mankind toward improvement, thus working to the disadvantage of posterity—that is absolutely forbidden. For himself (and only for a short time) a man may postpone enlightenment in what he ought to know, but to renounce it for himself and even more to renounce it for posterity is to injure and trample on the rights of mankind.

40   And what a people may not decree for itself can even less be decreed for them by a monarch, for his law-giving authority rests on his uniting the general public will in his own. If he only sees to it that all true or alleged improvement stands together with civil order, he can leave it to his subjects to do what they find necessary for their spiritual welfare. This is not his concern, though it is incumbent on him to prevent one of them from violently hindering another in determining and promoting this welfare to the best of his ability. To meddle in these matters lowers his own majesty, since by the writings in which his subjects seek to present their views he may evaluate his own governance. He can do this when, with deepest understanding, he lays upon himself the reproach, "Caesar non est supra grammaticos."[3] Far more does he injure his own majesty when he degrades his supreme power by supporting the ecclesiastical despotism of some tyrants in his state over his other subjects.

If we are asked, "Do we now live in an *enlightened age?*" the answer is, "No," but we do live in an *age of enlightenment.*[4] As things now stand, much is lacking which prevents men from being, or easily becoming, capable of correctly using their own reason in religious matters with assurance and free

---

[3] ["The emperor is not above the grammarians." Perhaps an allusion to a response to Voltaire said to have been made by Frederick the Great: "Caesar est supra grammaticam." But the sentiment was not original with Frederick, and has been attributed to the Emperor Sigismund at the Council of Constance (1414): "Ego sum rex Romanus et supra grammaticam."]

[4] ["Our age is, in especial degree, the age of criticism, and to criticism everything must submit" (*Critique of Pure Reason*, Preface to first edn., Smith trans.]

from outside direction. But, on the other hand, we have clear indications that the field has now been opened wherein men may freely deal with these things and that the obstacles to general enlightenment or the release from self-imposed tutelage are gradually being reduced. In this respect, this is the age of enlightenment, or the century of Frederick.

A prince who does not find it unworthy of himself to say that he holds it to be his duty to prescribe nothing to men in religious matters but to give them complete freedom while renouncing the haughty name of *tolerance,* is himself enlightened and deserves to be esteemed by the grateful world and posterity as the first, at least from the side of government, who divested the human race of its tutelage and left each man free to make use of his reason in matters of conscience. Under him venerable ecclesiastics are allowed, in the role of scholars, and without infringing on their official duties, freely to submit for public testing their judgments and views which here and there diverge from the established symbol. And an even greater freedom is enjoyed by those who are restricted by no official duties. This spirit of freedom spreads beyond this land, even to those in which it must struggle with external obstacles erected by a government which misunderstands its own interest. For an example gives evidence to such a government that in freedom there is not the least cause for concern about public peace and the stability of the community. Men work themselves gradually out of barbarity if only intentional artifices are not made to hold them in it.

I have placed the main point of enlightenment—the escape of men from their self-incurred tutelage—chiefly in matters of religion because our rulers have no interest in playing the guardian with respect to the arts and sciences and also because religious incompetence is not only the most harmful but also the most degrading of all. But the manner of thinking of the head of a state who favors religious enlightenment goes further, and he sees that there is no danger to his law-giving in allowing his subjects to make public use of their reason and to publish their thoughts on a better formulation of his legislation and even their open-minded criticisms of the laws already made. Of this we have a shining example wherein no monarch is superior to him whom we honor.

But only one who is himself enlightened is not afraid of shadows, and who has a numerous and well-disciplined army to assure public peace, can say: "Argue as much as you will, and about what you will, only obey!" A republic could not dare say such a thing. Here is shown a strange and unexpected trend in human affairs in which almost everything, looked at in the large, is paradoxical. A greater degree of civil freedom appears advantageous to the freedom of mind of the people, and yet it places inescapable limitations upon it; a lower degree of civil freedom, on the contrary, provides the mind with room for each man to extend himself to his full capacity. As nature has uncovered from under this hard shell the seed for which she most tenderly cares—the propensity and vocation to free thinking—this gradually works back upon the character of the people, who thereby gradually become capable of managing freedom; finally, it affects the principles of government, which finds it to its advantage to treat men, who are now more than machines, in accordance with their dignity.[5]

42

[5] Today I read in the *Büschingsche Wöchentliche Nachrichten* for September 13 an announcement of the *Berlinische Monatsschrift* for this month, which cites the answer to the same question by Mr. Mendelssohn.* But this issue has not yet come to me; if it had, I would have held back the present essay, which is now put forth only in order to see how much agreement in thought can be brought about by chance.

    * [Mendelssohn's answer was that enlightenment lay in intellectual cultivation, which he distinguished from the practical. Kant, quite in line with his later essay on theory and practice, refuses to make this distinction fundamental.]

IDEA FOR A UNIVERSAL HISTORY FROM A COSMOPOLITAN POINT OF VIEW[1]

Whatever concept one may hold, from a metaphysical point of view, concerning the freedom of the will, certainly its appearances, which are human actions, like every other natural event are determined by universal laws. However obscure their causes, history, which is concerned with narrating these appearances, permits us to hope that if we attend to the play of freedom of the human will in the large, we may be able to discern a regular movement in it, and that what seems complex and chaotic in the single individual may be seen from the standpoint of the human race as a whole to be a steady and progressive though slow evolution of its original endowment. Since the free will of man has obvious influence upon marriages, births, and deaths, they seem to be subject to no rule by which the number of them could be reckoned in advance. Yet the annual tables of them in the major countries prove that they occur according to laws as stable as [those of] the unstable weather, which we likewise cannot determine in advance, but which, in the large, maintain the growth of plants, the flow of rivers, and other natural events in an unbroken, uniform course. Individuals and even whole peoples think little on this. Each, according to his own inclination, follows his own purpose, often in opposition to others; yet each individual

---

[1] A statement in the "Short Notices" or the twelfth number of the *Gothaische Gelehrte Zeitung* of this year [1784], which no doubt was based on my conversation with a scholar who was traveling through, occasions this essay, without which that statement could not be understood.

[The notice said: "A favorite idea of Professor Kant's is that the ultimate purpose of the human race is to achieve the most perfect civic constitution, and he wishes that a philosophical historian might undertake to give us a history of humanity from this point of view, and to show to what extent humanity in various ages has approached or drawn away from this final purpose and what remains to be done in order to reach it."]

11

and people, as if following some guiding thread, go toward a natural but to each of them unknown goal; all work toward furthering it, even if they would set little store by it if they did know it.

Since men in their endeavors behave, on the whole, not just instinctively, like the brutes, nor yet like rational citizens of the world according to some agreed-on plan, no history of man conceived according to a plan seems to be possible, as it might be possible to have such a history of bees or beavers. One cannot suppress a certain indignation when one sees men's actions on the great world-stage and finds, beside the wisdom that appears here and there among individuals, everything in the large woven together from folly, childish vanity, even from childish malice and destructiveness. In the end, one does not know what to think of the human race, so conceited in its gifts. Since the philosopher cannot presuppose any [conscious] individual purpose among men in their great drama, there is no other expedient for him except to try to see if he can discover a natural purpose in this idiotic course of things human. In keeping with this purpose, it might be possible to have a history with a definite natural plan for creatures who have no plan of their own.

We wish to see if we can succeed in finding a clue to such a history; we leave it to Nature to produce the man capable of composing it. Thus Nature produced Kepler, who subjected, in an unexpected way, the eccentric paths of the planets to definite laws; and she produced Newton, who explained these laws by a universal natural cause.

FIRST THESIS

All natural capacities of a creature are destined to evolve completely to their natural end.

Observation of both the outward form and inward structure of all animals confirms this of them. An organ that is of no use, an arrangement that does not achieve its purpose, are contradictions in the teleological theory of nature. If we give up this fundamental principle, we no longer have a lawful but an aimless course of nature, and blind chance takes the place of the guiding thread of reason.

SECOND THESIS

In man (as the only rational creature on earth) *those natural capacities which are directed to the use of his reason are to be fully developed only in the race, not in the individual.*

Reason in a creature is a faculty of widening the rules and purposes of the use of all its powers far beyond natural instinct; it acknowledges no limits to its projects. Reason itself does not work instinctively, but requires trial, practice, and instruction in order gradually to progress from one level of insight to another. Therefore a single man would have to live excessively long in order to learn to make full use of all his natural capacities. Since Nature has set only a short period for his life, she needs a perhaps unreckonable series of generations, each of which passes its own enlightenment to its successor in order finally to bring the seeds of enlightenment to that degree of development in our race which is completely suitable to Nature's purpose. This point of time must be, at least as an ideal, the goal of man's efforts, for otherwise his natural capacities would have to be counted as for the most part vain and aimless. This would destroy all practical principles, and Nature, whose wisdom must serve as the fundamental principle in judging all her other offspring, would thereby make man alone a contemptible plaything.

19

THIRD THESIS

Nature has willed that man should, by himself, produce everything that goes beyond the mechanical ordering of his animal existence, and that he should partake of no other happiness or perfection than that which he himself, independently of instinct, has created by his own reason.

Nature does nothing in vain, and in the use of means to her

goals she is not prodigal. Her giving to man reason and the freedom of the will which depends upon it is clear indication of her purpose. Man accordingly was not to be guided by instinct, not nurtured and instructed with ready-made knowledge; rather, he should bring forth everything out of his own resources. Securing his own food, shelter, safety and defense (for which Nature gave him neither the horns of the bull, nor the claws of the lion, nor the fangs of the dog, but hands only), all amusement which can make life pleasant, insight and intelligence, finally even goodness of heart—all this should be wholly his own work. In this, Nature seems to have moved with the strictest parsimony, and to have measured her animal gifts precisely to the most stringent needs of a beginning existence, just as if she had willed that, if man ever did advance from the lowest barbarity to the highest skill and mental perfection and thereby worked himself up to happiness (so far as it is possible on earth), he alone should have the credit and should have only himself to thank—exactly as if she aimed more at his rational self-esteem than at his well-being. For along this march of human affairs, there was a host of troubles awaiting him. But it seems not to have concerned Nature that he should live well, but only that he should work himself upward so as to make himself, through his own actions, worthy of life and of well-being.

It remains strange that the earlier generations appear to carry through their toilsome labor only for the sake of the later, to prepare for them a foundation on which the later generations could erect the higher edifice which was Nature's goal, and yet that only the latest of the generations should have the good fortune to inhabit the building on which a long line of their ancestors had (unintentionally) labored without being permitted to partake of the fortune they had prepared. However puzzling this may be, it is necessary if one assumes that a species of animals should have reason, and, as a class of rational beings each of whom dies while the species is immortal, should develop their capacities to perfection.

FOURTH THESIS

The means employed by Nature to bring about the develop-
ment of all the capacities of men is their antagonism in society,
so far as this is, in the end, the cause of a lawful order among
men.

By "antagonism" I mean the unsocial sociability of men,
i.e., their propensity to enter into society, bound together with
a mutual opposition which constantly threatens to break up
the society. Man has an inclination to associate with others,
because in society he feels himself to be more than man, i.e.,   21
as more than the developed form of his natural capacities. But
he also has a strong propensity to isolate himself from others,
because he finds in himself at the same time the unsocial characteristic of wishing to have everything go according to his own
wish. Thus he expects opposition on all sides because, in knowing himself, he knows that he, on his own part, is inclined to
oppose others. This opposition it is which awakens all his
powers, brings him to conquer his inclination to laziness
and, propelled by vainglory, lust for power, and avarice, to
achieve a rank among his fellows whom he cannot tolerate but
from whom he cannot withdraw. Thus are taken the first true
steps from barbarism to culture, which consists in the social
worth of man; thence gradually develop all talents, and taste
is refined; through continued enlightenment the beginnings
are laid for a way of thought which can in time convert the
coarse, natural disposition for moral discrimination into definite practical principles, and thereby change a society of men
driven together by their natural feelings into a moral whole.
Without those in themselves unamiable characteristics of unsociability from whence opposition springs—characteristics
each man must find in his own selfish pretensions—all talents
would remain hidden, unborn in an Arcadian shepherd's life,
with all its concord, contentment, and mutual affection. Men,
good-natured as the sheep they herd, would hardly reach a
higher worth than their beasts; they would not fill the empty

place in creation by achieving their end, which is rational nature. Thanks be to Nature, then, for the incompatibility, for heartless competitive vanity, for the insatiable desire to possess and to rule! Without them, all the excellent natural capacities of humanity would forever sleep, undeveloped. Man wishes concord; but Nature knows better what is good for the race; she wills discord. He wishes to live comfortably and pleasantly; Nature wills that he should be plunged from sloth and passive contentment into labor and trouble, in order that he may find means of extricating himself from them. The natural urges to this, the sources of unsociableness and mutual opposition from which so many evils arise, drive men to new exertions of their forces and thus to the manifold development 22 of their capacities. They thereby perhaps show the ordering of a wise Creator and not the hand of an evil spirit, who bungled in his great work or spoiled it out of envy.

FIFTH THESIS

The greatest problem for the human race, to the solution of which Nature drives man, is the achievement of a universal civic society which administers law among men.

The highest purpose of Nature, which is the development of all the capacities which can be achieved by mankind, is attainable only in society, and more specifically in the society with the greatest freedom. Such a society is one in which there is mutual opposition among the members, together with the most exact definition of freedom and fixing of its limits so that it may be consistent with the freedom of others. Nature demands that humankind should itself achieve this goal like all its other destined goals. Thus a society in which freedom under external laws is associated in the highest degree with irresistible power, i.e., a perfectly just civic constitution, is the highest problem Nature assigns to the human race; for Nature can achieve her other purposes for mankind only upon the solution and completion of this assignment. Need forces men, so enamored otherwise of their boundless freedom, into this state of constraint. They are forced to it by the greatest of all needs, a need they themselves occasion inasmuch as their passions keep them from living long together in wild freedom. Once in such a preserve as a civic union, these same passions subsequently do the most good. It is just the same with trees in a forest: each needs the others, since each in seeking to take the air and sunlight from others must strive upward, and thereby each realizes a beautiful, straight stature, while those that live in isolated freedom put out branches at random and grow stunted, crooked, and twisted. All culture, art which adorns mankind, and the finest social order are fruits of unsociableness, which forces itself to discipline itself and so, by a contrived art, to develop the natural seeds to perfection.

SIXTH THESIS   23

This problem is the most difficult and the last to be solved by mankind.

The difficulty which the mere thought of this problem puts before our eyes is this. Man is an animal which, if it lives among others of its kind, requires a master. For he certainly abuses his freedom with respect to other men, and although as a reasonable being he wishes to have a law which limits the freedom of all, his selfish animal impulses tempt him, where possible, to exempt himself from them. He thus requires a master, who will break his will and force him to obey a will that is universally valid, under which each can be free. But whence does he get this master? Only from the human race. But then the master is himself an animal, and needs a master. Let him begin it as he will, it is not to be seen how he can procure a magistracy which can maintain public justice and which is itself just, whether it be a single person or a group of several elected persons. For each of them will always abuse his freedom if he has none above him to exercise force in accord with the laws. The highest master should be just in himself, and yet a man. This task is therefore the hardest of all; indeed, its complete solution is impossible, for from such crooked wood as man is made of, nothing perfectly straight can be built.[2] That it is the last problem to be solved follows also from this: it requires that there be a correct conception of a possible constitution, great experience gained in many paths of life, and—far beyond these—a good will ready to accept such a constitution. Three such things are very hard, and if they are ever to be found together, it will be very late and after many vain attempts.

24   SEVENTH THESIS

The problem of establishing a perfect civic constitution is dependent upon the problem of a lawful external relation among states and cannot be solved without a solution of the latter problem.

What is the use of working toward a lawful civic constitution among individuals, i.e., toward the creation of a commonwealth? The same unsociability which drives man to this causes any single commonwealth to stand in unrestricted freedom in relation to others; consequently, each of them must expect from another precisely the evil which oppressed the individuals and forced them to enter into a lawful civic state. The friction among men, the inevitable antagonism, which is a mark of even the largest societies and political bodies, is used by Nature as a means to establish a condition of quiet and security. Through war, through the taxing and never-ending accumulation of armament, through the want which any state, even in peacetime, must suffer internally, Nature forces them to make at first inadequate and tentative attempts; finally, after devastations, revolutions, and even complete exhaustion, she brings them to that which reason could have told them at the begin-

[2] The role of man is very artificial. How it may be with the dwellers on other planets and their nature we do not know. If, however, we carry out well the mandate given us by Nature, we can perhaps flatter ourselves that we may claim among our neighbors in the cosmos no mean rank. Maybe among them each individual can perfectly attain his destiny in his own life. Among us, it is different; only the race can hope to attain it.

ning and with far less sad experience, to wit, to step from the lawless condition of savages into a league of nations. In a league of nations, even the smallest state could expect security and justice, not from its own power and by its own decrees, but only from this great league of nations (*Foedus Amphictyonum* [3]), from a united power acting according to decisions reached under the laws of their united will. However fantastical this idea may seem—and it was laughed at as fantastical by the Abbé de St. Pierre [4] and by Rousseau,[5] perhaps because they believed it was too near to realization—the necessary outcome of the destitution to which each man is brought by his fellows is to force the states to the same decision (hard though it be for them) that savage man also was reluctantly forced to take, namely, to give up their brutish freedom and to seek quiet and security under a lawful constitution.

All wars are accordingly so many attempts (not in the intention of man, but in the intention of Nature) to establish new relations among states, and through the destruction or at least the dismemberment of all of them to create new political bodies, which, again, either internally or externally, cannot maintain themselves and which must thus suffer like revolutions; until finally, through the best possible civic constitution and common agreement and legislation in external affairs, a state is created which, like a civic commonwealth, can maintain itself automatically.

[There are three questions here, which really come to one.] Would it be expected from an Epicurean concourse of efficient causes that states, like minute particles of matter in their chance contacts, should form all sorts of unions which in their turn are destroyed by new impacts, until once, finally, by

25

3 [An allusion to the Amphictyonic League, a league of Greek tribes originally for the protection of a religious shrine, which later gained considerable political power.]

4 [Charles-Irénée Castel, Abbé de Saint Pierre (1658-1743), in his *Projet de paix perpetuelle* (Utrecht, 1713). Trans. H. H. Bellot (London, 1927).]

5 [In his *Extrait du projet de paix perpetuelle de M. l'Abbé de St. Pierre* (1760). Trans. C. E. Vaughn, *A Lasting Peace through the Federation of Europe* (London, 1917).]

chance a structure should arise which could maintain its existence—a fortunate accident that could hardly occur? Or are we
not rather to suppose that Nature here follows a lawful course
in gradually lifting our race from the lower levels of animality
to the highest level of humanity, doing this by her own secret
art, and developing in accord with her law all the original
gifts of man in this apparently chaotic disorder? Or perhaps
we should prefer to conclude that, from all these actions and
counteractions of men in the large, absolutely nothing, at least
nothing wise, is to issue? That everything should remain as it
always was, that we cannot therefore tell but that discord,
natural to our race, may not prepare for us a hell of evils,
however civilized we may now be, by annihilating civilization
and all cultural progress through barbarous devastation? (This
is the fate we may well have to suffer under the rule of blind
chance—which is in fact identical with lawless freedom—if
there is no secret wise guidance in Nature.) These three questions, I say, mean about the same as this: Is it reasonable to
assume a purposiveness in all the parts of nature and to deny
it to the whole?

Purposeless savagery held back the development of the capacities of our race; but finally, through the evil into which it
plunged mankind, it forced our race to renounce this condi-
26   tion and to enter into a civic order in which those capacities
could be developed. The same is done by the barbaric freedom
of established states. Through wasting the powers of the com-
monwealths in armaments to be used against each other,
through devastation brought on by war, and even more by the
necessity of holding themselves in constant readiness for war,
they stunt the full development of human nature. But because
of the evils which thus arise, our race is forced to find, above
the (in itself healthy) opposition of states which is a consequence of their freedom, a law of equilibrium and a united
power to give it effect. Thus it is forced to institute a cosmopolitan condition to secure the external safety of each state.

Such a condition is not unattended by the danger that the
vitality of mankind may fall asleep; but it is at least not with-

out a principle of balance among men's actions and counter-actions, without which they might be altogether destroyed. Until this last step to a union of states is taken, which is the halfway mark in the development of mankind, human nature must suffer the cruelest hardships under the guise of external well-being; and Rousseau was not far wrong in preferring the state of savages, so long, that is, as the last stage to which the human race must climb is not attained.

To a high degree we are, through art and science, *cultured*. We are *civilized*—perhaps too much for our own good—in all sorts of social grace and decorum. But to consider ourselves as having reached *morality*—for that, much is lacking. The ideal of morality belongs to culture; its use for some simulacrum of morality in the love of honor and outward decorum constitutes mere civilization. So long as states waste their forces in vain and violent self-expansion, and thereby constantly thwart the slow efforts to improve the minds of their citizens by even withdrawing all support from them, nothing in the way of a moral order is to be expected. For such an end, a long internal working of each political body toward the education of its citizens is required. Everything good that is not based on a morally good disposition, however, is nothing but pretense and glittering misery. In such a condition the human species will no doubt remain until, in the way I have described, it works its way out of the chaotic conditions of its international relations.

EIGHTH THESIS   27

The history of mankind can be seen, in the large, as the realization of Nature's secret plan to bring forth a perfectly constituted state as the only condition in which the capacities of mankind can be fully developed, and also bring forth that external relation among states which is perfectly adequate to this end.

This is a corollary to the preceding. Everyone can see that philosophy can have her belief in a millenium, but her millenarianism is not Utopian, since the Idea can help, though only from afar, to bring the millenium to pass. The only question is: Does Nature reveal anything of a path to this end? And I say: She reveals something, but very little. This great revolution seems to require so long for its completion that the short period during which humanity has been following this course permits us to determine its path and the relation of the parts to the whole with as little certainty as we can determine, from all previous astronomical observation, the path of the sun and his host of satellites among the fixed stars. Yet, on the fundamental premise of the systematic structure of the cosmos and from the little that has been observed, we can confidently infer the reality of such a revolution.

Moreover, human nature is so constituted that we cannot be indifferent to the most remote epoch our race may come to, if only we may expect it with certainty. Such indifference is even less possible for us, since it seems that our own intelligent action may hasten this happy time for our posterity. For that reason, even faint indications of approach to it are very important to us. At present, states are in such an artificial relation to each other that none of them can neglect its internal cultural development without losing power and influence among the others. Therefore the preservation of this natural end [culture], if not progress in it, is fairly well assured by the ambitions of states. Furthermore, civic freedom can hardly be infringed without the evil consequences being felt in all walks 28 of life, especially in commerce, where the effect is loss of power of the state in its foreign relations. But this freedom spreads by degrees. When the citizen is hindered in seeking his own welfare in his own way, so long as it is consistent with the freedom of others, the vitality of the entire enterprise is sapped, and therewith the powers of the whole are diminished. Therefore limitations on personal actions are step by step removed, and general religious freedom is permitted. Enlightenment comes gradually, with intermittent folly and caprice, as a great good which must finally save men from the selfish aggrandizement of their masters, always assuming that the latter know their own interest. This enlightenment, and with it a certain commitment of heart which the enlightened man cannot fail to make to the good he clearly understands, must step by step ascend the throne and influence the principles of government.

Although, for instance, our world rulers at present have no money left over for public education and for anything that concerns what is best in the world, since all they have is already committed to future wars, they will still find it to their own interest at least not to hinder the weak and slow, independent efforts of their peoples in this work. In the end, war itself will be seen as not only so artificial, in outcome so uncertain for both sides, in aftereffects so painful in the form of an ever-growing war debt (a new invention) that cannot be met, that it will be regarded as a most dubious undertaking. The impact of any revolution on all states on our continent, so closely knit together through commerce, will be so obvious that the other states, driven by their own danger but without any legal basis, will offer themselves as arbiters, and thus they will prepare the way for a distant international government for which there is no precedent in world history. Although this government at present exists only as a rough outline, nevertheless in all the members there is rising a feeling which each has for the preservation of the whole. This gives hope finally that after many reformative revolutions, a universal cosmopolitan condition, which Nature has as her ultimate purpose, will come into being as the womb wherein all the original capacities of the human race can develop.

NINTH THESIS   29

A philosophical attempt to work out a universal history according to a natural plan directed to achieving the civic union of the human race must be regarded as possible and, indeed, as contributing to this end of Nature.

It is strange and apparently silly to wish to write a history in accordance with an Idea [6] of how the course of the world must be if it is to lead to certain rational ends. It seems that with such an Idea only a romance could be written. Nevertheless, if one may assume that Nature, even in the play of human freedom, works not without plan or purpose, this Idea could still be of use. Even if we are too blind to see the secret mechanism of its workings, this Idea may still serve as a guiding thread for presenting as a system, at least in broad outlines, what would otherwise be a planless conglomeration of human actions. For if one starts with Greek history, through which every older or contemporaneous history has been handed down or at least certified; [7] if one follows the influence of Greek history on the construction and misconstruction of the Roman state which swallowed up the Greek, then the Roman influence on the barbarians who in turn destroyed it, and so on down to our times; if one adds episodes from the national histories of other peoples insofar as they are known from the history of the enlightened nations, one will discover a regular progress in the constitution of states on our continent (which will probably give law, eventually, to all the others). If, further, one concentrates on the civic constitutions and their laws and on the relations among states, insofar as through the good they contained they served over long periods of time to elevate and adorn nations and their arts and sciences, while through the evil they

[6] [For the Kantian sense of "Idea," see Introduction, p. xix and note 15.]

[7] Only a learned public, which has lasted from its beginning to our own day, can certify ancient history. Outside it, everything else is *terra incognita;* and the history of peoples outside it can only be begun when they come into contact with it. This happened with the Jews in the time of the Ptolemies through the translation of the Bible into Greek, without which we would give little credence to their isolated narratives. From this point, when once properly fixed, we can retrace their history. And so with all other peoples. The first page of Thucydides, says Hume,* is the only beginning of all real history.

* ["Of the Populousness of Ancient Nations," in *Essays Moral, Political, and Literary,* eds. Green and Grose, Vol. I, p. 414.]

contained they destroyed them, if only a germ of enlightenment was left to be further developed by this overthrow and a
higher level was thus prepared—if, I say, one carries through
this study, a guiding thread will be revealed. It can serve not
only for clarifying the confused play of things human, and not
only for the art of prophesying later political changes (a use
which has already been made of history even when seen as the
disconnected effect of lawless freedom), but for giving a con-
soling view of the future (which could not be reasonably hoped
for without the presupposition of a natural plan) in which
there will be exhibited in the distance how the human race
finally achieves the condition in which all the seeds planted in
it by Nature can fully develop and in which the destiny of the
race can be fulfilled here on earth.

Such a justification of Nature—or, better, of Providence—is
no unimportant reason for choosing a standpoint toward
world history. For what is the good of esteeming the majesty
and wisdom of Creation in the realm of brute nature and of
recommending that we contemplate it, if that part of the great
stage of supreme wisdom which contains the purpose of all the
others—the history of mankind—must remain an unceasing reproach to it? If we are forced to turn our eyes from it in dis-
gust, doubting that we can ever find a perfectly rational purpose in it and hoping for that only in another world?

That I would want to displace the work of practicing empirical historians with this Idea of world history, which is to
some extent based upon an a priori principle, would be a mis-
interpretation of my intention. It is only a suggestion of what
a philosophical mind (which would have to be well versed in
history) could essay from another point of view. Otherwise the
notorious complexity of a history of our time must naturally
lead to serious doubt as to how our descendants will begin to
grasp the burden of the history we shall leave to them after a
few centuries. They will naturally value the history of earlier 31
times, from which the documents may long since have disappeared, only from the point of view of what interests them, i.e.,

in answer to the question of what the various nations and governments have contributed to the goal of world citizenship, and what they have done to damage it. To consider this, so as to direct the ambitions of sovereigns and their agents to the only means by which their fame can be spread to later ages: this can be a minor motive for attempting such a philosophical history.

REVIEWS OF HERDER'S
IDEAS FOR A PHILOSOPHY OF THE HISTORY OF MANKIND

I

Ideas for a Philosophy of the History of Mankind by Joh. Gottfr. Herder. *Quem te Deus esse iussit et humana qua parte locatus es in re disce.*[1] Part One. 318 pages. 4⁰. Hartknoch: Riga and Leipzig, 1784.

Our ingenious and eloquent author demonstrates his already   45 renowned individuality in this publication. It can therefore be judged as little according to ordinary standards as many others from his prolific pen. It is as if his genius did not simply assemble ideas out of the wide range of arts and sciences in order to add them to other intelligible ideas, but as if he transformed them according to a certain law of assimilation (to borrow his own expression) peculiar to him in his particular manner of thinking. Thus they are markedly differentiated from those through which other minds are nourished and thrive (p. 292) and thus become less capable of being communicated. Hence what philosophy of the history of humanity means to him may very well be something quite different from what is normally understood under that name. His is not a logical precision in the definition of concepts or careful adherence to principles, but rather a fleeting, sweeping view, an adroitness in unearthing analogies in the wielding of which he shows a bold imagination. This is combined with cleverness in soliciting sympathy for his subject—kept in increasingly hazy remoteness— by means of sentiment and sensation. Further suspicion is stimulated as to whether these emotions are effects of a prodigious

---

1 ["Learn what God has commanded you to be and what role he has assigned to you." Persius, *Satire* III. 11, 12. This is Herder's proem.]

27

system of thought or only equivocal hints which cool, critical examination would uncover in them. Nevertheless, since freedom of thought (which is encountered here in quantity) practiced by a productive mind always provides food for thought, we want to seek, as far as it will profit us, to select from the ideas themselves his most important and characteristic ones and present them in his own terms; then finally we will add some remarks concerning the whole.

46   Our author commences by enlarging the horizon in order to point out to man his position among the inhabitants of the planets of our solar system. Considering the sphere, centrally and advantageously situated, which man occupies, he concludes that there is only a "mediocre earthly faculty of understanding and a still more ambiguous ability upon which man has to rely. Our thoughts and abilities are obviously only products of our terrestrial constitution, and they strive to transform and transfigure themselves to the point of eventually attaining the purity and refinement that our creation is able to impart. And if analogy may be our guide, it would not be different on other stars. This allows the conjecture that man may have one goal in common with the inhabitants of other stars: in the end, not only to embark upon a journey to other celestial bodies, but perhaps also to enter into relations with all of the creatures who have reached a maturity in our sister-worlds so numerous and diverse." From there he goes on to view the revolutions which preceded the creation of man. "Prior to the appearance of our air, water, and earth, many forces, opposing and releasing one another, were necessary. And how many transformations and revolutions, one into the next, of the multifarious species of the earth—minerals, crystallizations, even the organization into shell-fish, plants, animals and finally into man— were not presupposed? [2] He, the son of all elements and con-

---

[2] [Thus far the passage has been misquoted. In the definitive edition of the work, Vols. XIII and XIV of *Herders Sämmtliche Werke* published by Bernhard Suphan, Berlin, 1887, the passage reads: "Many plants had to effloresce and perish before an animal organism came into existence; insects, primitive aerial and aquatic creatures, and beasts of the night also

ditions, their epitome, and, as it were, the flower of earth's creation—he could be nothing less than the ultimate favorite child of nature, whose formation and reception had to be preceded by many developments and revolutions."

The spherical shape of the earth offers our author another object of wonder for the unity which it manifests in spite of all its imaginable diversity. "Having once pondered this figure, which of you would have allowed yourselves to fall into philosophic and religious orthodoxies or, with lurid but holy zeal, commit murder in their name?" Even the slant of the ecliptic provides him occasion for an opinion on human destiny: "Under our obliquely moving sun all human activity occurs in yearly cycles." [3] Greater knowledge of the atmosphere and even the influence of the heavenly bodies upon it, if it were understood better, seem to him to promise a profound influence on human history. In the section dealing with the distribution of the lands and seas, the configuration of the earth is presented as an explanatory principle of the difference in the history of peoples. "Asia is as homogeneous in manners and morals as it is topographically uniform; the small Red Sea, on

47

---

preceded the refined creatures who dwell on the earth in the light of day. Finally, after all else, man appeared, the crowning glory of earthly creation, *microcosm*" (XIII, 23). Kant is therefore interpolating evolution into the thought, a notion that Herder expressly repudiated. There is nothing here of "transformations and revolutions, one into the next (*des Einen in das Andere*), of the multifarious species of the earth." In the very section which Kant is now criticizing, Herder writes: "*No creature that we know has transcended its original organization and violated it by preparing itself for another . . .*" (XIII, 114). Elsewhere he repeats: "Man and the ape were definitely never one and the same species. . . . Nature has formed each species well enough and given it its own heritage" (XIII, 257). Kant's case against Herder rests partly on imputing to him a defiling evolutionism.]

[3] [This statement does not appear in the work. See XIII, 18-21. Herder is simply trying to establish the intermediary position of the earth in the solar system, from which he concludes ". . . that perhaps the rays of the single Sun of the True and the Beautiful reach each planet from a different angle so that its entire usufruct could not be monopolized by a single one of them" (XII, 21).]

the other hand, already differentiates moral systems, and the Persian Gulf does so even more. But the land, lakes, mountains, and rivers of America were not of such a vast expanse in the temperate zone without a reason; and the structure of the old continent, the first habitat of man, was ordered differently by nature than in the new world."

The second book is concerned with terrestrial organizations. It begins with granite, upon which light, heat, harsh winds, and water have acted. These elements perhaps transformed silex into calcareous earth in which the first organic creatures of the sea, the crustaceans, were formed. Further along vegetation appears. Comparison of the formation of man with that of plants, and man's mode of sexual love with the florescence of flowers. Use of the plant realm in considering man. Animal realm. Transformation of animals and men according to climate. Those of the primeval world are imperfect. "The classes of creatures increase the further removed they are from man; the nearer to him, the fewer of them there are. . . . In everything there is an essential [*Haupt*] form, a similar bone structure. . . . These transitions suggest that in marine life, plants, perhaps even in extinct creatures, one and the same plan of organization may prevail, only infinitely more crude and confused. In the view of the eternal being who sees everything in a continuum, it is possible that the form of an icicle, in the process of creation, and the snowflake which forms in it, have an increasingly analogous relation to the development of the embryo in the womb. . . . Man is an intermediary creature among the animals, that is, the most inclusive form in which all characteristics of all species merge in the finest configuration. . . . Out of air and water, from the heights and the depths, as it were, I see the animals converge toward man and step by step approximate his form." This book closes: "Rejoice you at your rank, O man, and contemplate yourself, noble microcosm, in everything that dwells about you."

The third book compares the structure of the plants and animals with the human organism. Since he resorts here to the naturalist's mode of thinking for his purpose, we cannot fol-

low him. Just a few results: "Through various organs the creature generates living excitation out of dead vegetation, and   48
out of the sum of this, the medium of sensation, purified
through fine canals. The result of excitation is instinct and the
result of sensation is thought; there is an eternal progression
[Fortgang] 4 of organic creation which inheres in every living
thing." The author does not begin with origins but rather with
an organic force, in plants as well as in animals. He says: "Just
as the plant itself is organic life, so is the polyp. Thus there
are many organic forces, those of vegetation, muscular excitation, and sensation. The more nerves there are, and the finer
they are, the larger the brain is, and the more intelligent becomes the species. The animal mind is the sum of all the forces
acting in an organism, and instinct is not a distinct force of
nature but the direction that nature gave to that constellation
of forces by means of its temperature. The more that an organic
principle of nature—a principle called either *formative* (in
minerals), *irritative* (in plants), *sensible,* or *inventive,* and
which is basically only one and the same organic force—is divided into various organs and different members, the more it
forms in each of them a separate world; and the more does
instinct disappear and a free, individual use of limbs and intelligence begin (as in man)." Finally the author comes to the
essential natural distinctions of mankind. "The erect gait of
man is natural to him alone; indeed, it is the posture proper to
the whole calling of his race and also his distinguishing character."

Upright posture and the rational use of his limbs were not
allotted to man because he was destined to be a rational creature; on the contrary, he acquired reason by virtue of his erect
stature, as the natural effect of that stature which was necessary merely to make him walk upright. "Let us linger a moment before this august work of art, this beneficence [*Wohltat*]
to which our race owes its human character; let us gaze with
wonder and admiration as we ponder the new organization of

4 [*Fortgang* means progression and denotes development, but the word
is not equivalent to evolution in Darwin's sense.]

forces which originated in the erect posture and see that
through it alone man became man!"

In the fourth book the author pursues this point further.
"What does that creature resembling man (the ape) lack, that
he did not become human"—and how did man emerge?
Through the conformation of the head to an erect stature by
means of inner and outer organization around a perpendicular
center of gravity: the ape has all of the parts of the brain
49 which the human possesses; he has them, however, because of
the shape of his cranium, in a depressed position. This was the
result of the fact that his head was formed to a different angle
and he was not made for an erect gait. Forthwith all of his
organic powers acted differently. "Lift your gaze heavenward,
O man, and rejoice at your immeasurable excellence which the
world-creator connected to such an elementary principle, your
upright figure. Raised above the ground and foliage, scent
no longer governs, but the eye. . . . Given erect posture, man
became an artistic creation endowed with free and inventive
hands, and only in the erect carriage does true human language appear. . . . Both from the theoretical and practical
points of view, reason is simply an acquisition, something
learned, a proportion and orientation of ideas and abilities to
which man was fashioned by his structure and mode of life."
And now freedom: "The human being is the first freedman in
creation; he stands upright." And then modesty: "Modesty
soon developed, given the upright form." His nature is subjected to no special variety. "How is this so? By virtue of his
upright form and nothing else. . . . He is formed for humanity
[Humanität]: peaceableness, sexual love, sympathy, maternal
love—all an outgrowth of the erectness of humanity. The rule
of justice and truth is grounded in that same uprightness which
also fashions man for virtue [Wohlanständigkeit]; religion is
the supreme expression of humanity. The prostrate animal
perceives only dimly; God raised man up in such a way that,
without knowing or choosing it, he might penetrate into the
origins of things and discover thee, thou great masterplan of
all things. Religion, however, advances hope and faith in im-

mortality." The fifth book speaks of this matter. "In the progression from minerals to crystals, from crystals to metals, from metals to vegetation, from that to the animal and finally to man, we saw the form of organization ascend, and at the same time the powers and instincts of the creature become more variegated; finally we observed all uniting in the form of man, as far as it could comprise them. . . ."

"Through this series of states we observed a similarity of principal [*Haupt*] forms which increasingly approached the human form; likewise we saw the powers and instincts approximate man. . . . The determination of the longevity of each creature is another function of nature and is performed with a definite end in view. The better organized a creature is, the more is its structure compounded out of lower realms. Man is a compendium of the world: lime, earth, salts, acids, 50 oils, and water, and the powers of vegetation, excitation, and sensation are organically united in him. . . . This induces us to accept also an invisible realm of forces, an ascending series of imperceptible powers, which maintains exactly the same relations and connections as the visible realm of creation does. . . . There is the *complete* explanation, not only for the immortality of the soul, but for the permanence of all active and animate forces of the created world. Force cannot perish even though its organ may be disarranged. Whatever the omnipresent life-giver summoned to life lives; whatever acts, acts eternally in the eternal scheme." These principles are not analyzed "because this is not the place for it." However, "In matter we observe so many spirit-like forces that a complete contrast and opposition between these two essences, spirit and matter, so very distinct, seems, if not self-contradictory, at least completely undemonstrated." "No eye has seen preformed embryos. If a person speaks of epigenesis he is speaking figuratively, as if limbs could be actuated from without. It is formation (genesis), an effect of inner energies; nature had prepared a mass which agglomerates them and through which they should make themselves visible. It is not our rational soul which forms the body, but the finger of divinity, organic force." Now that means: "(1) Force and organ are certainly most intimately united, yet they are not one and the same. (2) Each force acts in harmony with its organ, for it has formed the organ solely for the purpose of manifesting its essence and assimilating itself. (3) If the integument falls away the force remains that existed prior to it, although in a lower but still organic condition." Then the author addresses the materialists: "Admit that our soul is originally one and the same with all of the material forces, excitation, movement, vitality, and acts only on a higher plane in a finer and more developed form; for has anyone ever seen a force of movement or excitation decline, and are these lower forces coexistent with their organs?" The close connection between them proves that it can only be a case of progressive evolution [*Fortschreitung*]. "The human race can be viewed as the greatest confluence of lower organic forces which must have germinated in it for the cultivation of humanity [*Humanität*]."

51   That the human structure occurs in a realm of spiritual forces is demonstrated in the following way: "(1) Thought is a completely different thing from what sense conveys to it; all that we know of its origin leads to the belief that it is the effect of a truly organic but autonomous essence, which acts according to laws of spiritual association. (2) As the body increases through nourishment, so does the mind through ideas; indeed, in the mind we can even observe the laws of assimilation, growth, and procreation. In short, there is formed in us an inner, spiritual man who has his own peculiar nature and uses the body only as an implement. . . . The more lucid consciousness, this great excellence of the human soul, was first formed into an intellectual mode through *Humanität,* etc." In a word, if we understand aright, the soul emerged first of all from spiritual powers which are gradually augmented. "Our humanity is only preparation, the bud of a future flower. Step by step nature rejects what is base, and in exchange, cultivates the Spirit, urges what is fine into something still finer. And so we can hope that from her creative hand our bud of hu-

manity also will appear in yonder existence in its individual, true, divine, human form."

This passage states the conclusion: "The current condition of man is probably the intermediate stage between two worlds. . . . If man closes the chain of mundane structures as its final and highest member, at the same time he commences the chain of a yet higher class of creatures as its lowest member. Thus he is probably the middle link between two interlinking systems of creation. He represents two worlds in one to us and that accounts for the apparent duality of his essence. . . . Life is a battle; the flower of pure, immortal humanity a painfully acquired crown. Hence our brothers of the higher reaches can certainly love us more than we can seek and love them, for they see our condition more clearly, and they will educate us perhaps as fellow participants in their felicity. . . . It is probably not imaginable that the future state was meant to be so completely incommunicable to the present as the animal in man would like to believe; thus it seems that without higher guidance, language and primitive science are inexplicable. . . . Even in later times the greatest effects on earth have originated through incomprehensible circumstances; diseases themselves were often instruments for such ends when the organ proved useless for the normal round of earthly life. It seems natural thus that the inner, restless power perhaps receives impressions 52 of which an undisturbed structure was not capable. . . . Still man should not peer into his future situation, but just believe in it." (But how, if he once believes that he is able to gaze therein, can he be restrained from seeking to make use of this ability now and then?) "This much is certain, that in each of his powers lies an infinity; the forces of the universe, too, seem concealed in his soul, and only an organism, or a series of them, is required to allow it to pass over into actuality and exercise. . . . Just as the flower stood forth and terminated the realm of subterranean, still lifeless creation in an upright form, so stands man erect, in his turn, dominating the realms of prostrate earth-dwellers (the beasts). With lofty gaze and

uplifted hands he stands there as a son of the house awaiting
the summons of his father."

Supplement

The idea and final purpose of Part One (I say One as there
is the likelihood of several subsequent volumes of the work)
consist in the following. The spiritual nature of the human
soul, its permanence and progress toward perfection, is to be
proved by analogy with the natural forms of matter, particularly in their structure, with no recourse to metaphysics. For
this purpose, spiritual forces, a certain invisible domain of
creation, are assumed for which matter constitutes only the
framework. This realm contains the animating power which
organizes everything in such a way that the schema of the
perfection of this organic system is to be man. All earthly creatures, from the lowest level on, approximate him until finally,
through nothing else than this perfected organic system, of
which the essential condition is the upright gait of the animal,
man emerged. His death can never more terminate the progress
and enhancement of the structure already shown before so
copiously in all kinds of creatures. Rather a transcendence of
nature is expected to still more refined operations in order to
further him thereby to yet higher grades of life, and so continuously to promote and elevate him into infinitude.

The reviewer must confess that he still does not perceive this
53 chain of reasoning from the analogy of nature even if he were
willing to concede such a continuous gradation of its creatures
and rule that the gradations have a progressive approximation
to the human. For there are distinct beings here which occupy
the various stages of more and more perfect organic systems.
Thus it could only be concluded by such an analogy that some-
where else, perhaps on another planet, creatures may exist
anew offering the next higher stage of organization above man,
but not that the same individual would attain it. With flying
insects, which develop from larvae or grubs, we have quite a
peculiar arrangement, different from the typical natural proc-

ess; and even here palingenesis is to follow not death, but only the chrysalis stage. But contrary to this, it would have to be proved that nature elevated animals, even after their decomposition or combustion, from their ashes into specifically more consummate forms: then the same thing might be inferred by analogy with respect to man who is here transformed into ashes.

Hence there is not the least resemblance between the gradient progression in the very same man who is ever ascending to a more perfect structure in another life and the ladder which one may conceive among completely different types and individuals in the realm of nature. Here nature allows us to see nothing else than that it abandons individuals to complete destruction and only maintains the type. But then we demand to know if the soul of man will also survive his destruction here on earth; this can be concluded perhaps on moral—or if you like metaphysical—grounds, but never by any kind of analogy to visible creation. Moreover, whatever may be that imperceptible realm of active, autonomous powers, the following still presents a problem: why did not the author, after he believed he could infer the existence of this realm from organic creation, prefer to let the thinking principle in man derive from it directly, instead of lifting it out of chaos through the structure of organization? Unless he considered these spiritual forces as something quite different from the human soul, he should regard the soul, not as a special substance, but simply as an effect of an invisible, universal nature acting on matter and animating it. This is an opinion we hesitate out of fairness to attribute to him. But, in the first place, what should we think of this hypothesis of invisible forces acting on the organism; and then, how should we regard the design which aims 54 to explain that which one does not comprehend by that which one comprehends even less? As to the former, we can at least still recognize the law by means of experience, although, of course, the causes themselves remain unknown: but of the latter even experience is denied us. What can the philosopher now invoke here to justify his allegations except simple despair of finding clarification in some kind of knowledge of nature and the attendent necessity to seek it in the fertile field of the poetic imagination? But this is still metaphysics, and what is more, very dogmatic metaphysics, even though our author renounces it, as fashion demands.

However, as to the ladder of organization, we cannot reproach the author too much if it does not reach his goal which lies far above this world, for its utility with respect to the realm of nature here on earth likewise leads nowhere. If the species are established in succession according to their likeness, the minuteness of the distinctions, in the presence of such great diversity, is also a necessary consequence of this diversity. There is only one relationship among them, but this would lead to ideas which are so monstrous that reason recoils from them: either one species would have emerged out of the other and all out of one single original species, or perhaps all would have emerged out of a single primordial womb. Such ideas one cannot attribute to our author without being unjust. As to the contribution of these ideas to comparative anatomy in regard to all animal species as far down as the plant, it is for competent people to judge how far they may influence the description of nature and in what measure the direction they provide, in view of new observations, might be utilized, and also if this direction actually has some basis. But the unity of organic force (p. 141), as self-constituting with respect to the manifold of all organic creatures and as subsequently acting upon organs according to their differences so as to establish their many genera and species, is an Idea [5] which lies wholly outside the field of empirical natural science. This Idea of organic force belongs solely to speculative philosophy; but if it were to gain entry even there, it would cause great havoc among accepted conceptions. To want to determine what arrangement of the head, externally with respect to its shape, and internally with respect to its brain, is necessarily con-
55   nected with the propensity toward an upright posture; still more, to want to determine how a simple organization di-

[5] [For the Kantian sense of "Idea," see Introduction, p. xix and note 15.]

rected solely to this end could contain the ability to reason (a pursuit therefore in which the beast participates)—that patently exceeds all human reason. For reason, thus conceived, totters on the top rung of the physiological ladder and is on the point of taking metaphysical wing.

Despite these remonstrances all credit ought not be denied this very thoughtful work. There is one remarkable thing about it (not to mention here the reflections so eloquently expressed that they testify to noble and sincere thought): this is the courage with which its author knew how to overcome the suspicions of this profession with respect to unaided efforts of reason, the question of how far reason alone can accomplish its tasks—suspicions often restrictive of all philosophy. Apart from that, the mysterious obscurity in which nature herself envelopes the formation of organic systems and the classification of her creatures, deserves part of the blame for the obscurity and uncertainty which attaches to this first part of a philosophical human history. This section was conceived with the intention of conjoining wherever possible the most extreme ends: the point where human history begins and the point where it loses itself in the infinite reaches beyond world history.

To be sure, this attempt is bold but still natural to the scientific bent of our reason, and it should not pass uncommended despite an execution that is only partially successful. All the more is it to be wished, therefore, that our gifted author in continuing his work, where there is solid ground before him, should constrain his lively genius. It is to be hoped that philosophy, whose concern consists more in the pruning than the sprouting of superfluous growth, may guide him to the consummation of his enterprise, not with hints, but precise concepts, not through supposed, but through observed laws, not through the intervention of flighty imagination, whether metaphysical or sentimental, but rather through the exercise of careful reason in the execution of his bold project.

II

Rejoinder of the reviewer of Herder's *Ideas for a Philosophy
of the History of Mankind* (No. 4 and supplement of the
Allg. Lit. Zeit.) related to a writing in the February issue
of the *Teutscher Merkur* which attacks this review.

In the February issue of the *Teutscher Merkur* (p. 148), a
defender of Mr. Herder appears, signing himself as a clergyman, against the presumed attack in our *Allgemeine Liter-
arische Zeitung*. It would be unfair to involve the name of a
respected author in the dispute between reviewers and re-
butters; hence we only intend to justify our manner of proceeding in reviewing and appraising of the aforementioned
work according to the maxims of conscientiousness, impart-
iality, and moderation which this gazette has taken as its guide.
In his writing, the clergyman quarrels at length with a metaphysician whom he has in mind and who, as he presents him,
is completely refractory to all empirical methods of instruction, or, if this does not complete the matter, is insensitive to
inferences from the analogy of nature. This metaphysician, in
his view, would like to reduce everything to his sterile, scholastic abstractions. The reviewer can bypass this quarrel with
complete equanimity, for he is fully one with the clergyman
in this opinion, and the review itself is the best proof of that.
As the reviewer believes, however, that he knows pretty well
the materials involved in anthropology and also something of
its methods in undertaking a history of humanity in the whole
scope of its destiny, he is convinced that it must be sought
neither in metaphysics nor in the armory of specimens for
a natural history by means of the comparison of the skeleton
of man with that of other animal species. Least of all could
such a comparison inform us of man's destination in another
world; that can be found only in human actions through which
man manifests his character.

The reviewer is also convinced that Mr. Herder has not

once had the intention in the first part of his work (which simply presents man as an animal in the general system of nature and thereby reveals a premonitory symptom of future ideas) to furnish the real materials for a human history. He only intended to display thoughts which could attract the attention of the physiologists and to extend their research, which they generally turn only toward a mechanical view of the animal structure, to the organization appropriate to this creature for the use of reason. In so doing he has attributed more importance to this research than is justified. It is not even necessary that a person who shares this latter view (as the clergyman claims, p. 161) establish that human reason would even be possible in another organic form. For this can be as little proved as the notion that reason is possible only in the present form. The reasonable use of experience also has its limits. It can indeed teach us that something is constituted in such or such a way, but never that it absolutely cannot be anything else; nor can analogy fill this immense void between the contingent and the necessary. In our review it was said: "If the species are established in succession according to their likeness, then the minuteness of the distinctions, in the presence of such great diversity, is also a necessary consequence of this diversity. There is only one relationship among them, but this would lead to ideas which are so monstrous that reason recoils from them: either one species would have emerged out of the other or all would have emerged out of one single original species and perhaps out of a single primordial womb. Such ideas one cannot attribute to our author without being unjust." [6]

These words have misled the clergyman into believing that there is metaphysical orthodoxy and, consequently, intolerance in our review of the work. He asserts: *"The healthy reason, acting freely, recoils from no idea whatever."* But nothing that he fancies is to be feared. It is simply the *horror vacui* experienced by the common human reason which causes it to recoil

[6] [The wording here is slightly different from the original passage on p. 38 above.]

when an idea is encountered by means of which absolutely nothing can be thought. And from this point of view, the ontological codex might well serve as the canon of the theological codex directly in the interest of tolerance. Moreover the clergyman finds the merit we ascribed to the book for freedom of thought much too common for such a celebrated author. Undoubtedly he means by that the *external* freedom which, because it depends upon time and place, has no merit at all. But the review visualized that *inner* freedom which is unfettered by customary concepts and current modes of thought reinforced by public opinion, a freedom which is so utterly uncommon that even those who regard themselves as philosophers have only rarely been able to rise to it. What he reproaches in the review, *"that it lifts out passages which express the results, but at the same time omits the preparatory ones,"* may well be an unavoidable evil of authorship in general which, in spite of everything, however, is still more tolerable than to condemn or acclaim simply on the basis of an arbitrarily selected passage. Thus we reaffirm our judgment of the book in question which was passed with fair regard and even sympathy for the author's present fame, and still more for his future renown. How different it sounds from that which the clergyman foists upon him on p. 161 (not very responsibly), *that the book has not accomplished what its title promised.* The title, in fact, promised nothing at all, since the first volume only contains some general preparatory exercises in physiology, to provide that which we are anticipating from the following part (which, as far as can be judged, will contain actual anthropology). And the reminder was not amiss: to circumscribe freedom in the first which might well merit indulgence in the second. In any case it depends on the author himself to fulfill the claim of the title, and there is good reason to hope that with his talent and learning he will succeed.

III

Hartknoch: Riga and Leipzig. *Ideas for a Philosophy of the History of Mankind* by Johann Gottfried Herder. Part Two. 344 pages. 8°. 1785.

This part, extending to the tenth Book, first describes in six sections of Book Six the organization of the peoples in the vicinity of the North Pole as well as the Asian ridge of the earth, the zone of the civilized peoples, the African nations, the island populations in the torrid zone and the Americas.[7] The author concludes his description by expressing the desire for a collection of new portrayals of peoples, which Niebuhr, Parkinson, Cook, Höst, Georgi and others have already initiated. "What a fine gift it would be if someone who could would collect the faithful paintings scattered here and there which demonstrate the distinctiveness of our species and thus laid the foundations for an accurate theory and physiognomy of mankind.[8] Art could scarcely find a more philosophic application, and an anthropological chart, like the zoological chart that Zimmermann has attempted, on which nothing must be indicated except what makes for human diversity, but this considered in all of its aspects and manifestations—such a chart would crown the philanthropic work." 59

The seventh Book first of all considers the propositions that, in spite of such diverse forms, the human race nonetheless constitutes only one species everywhere, and that this single race has acclimatized itself everywhere in the world. After this, the effects of climate on the formation of man are examined. The author sagaciously observes that much preparatory work is still lacking to enable us to arrive at a physiological pathology, not to mention a climatology, of all the intellectual and sensory powers of man. There is a chaos of causes and effects, along

---

7 [Only the Indians are meant here.]

8 [This passage is slightly misquoted although the meaning is unchanged.]

with other circumstances, which determine the relief of a terrestrial zone, its contexture and products, food and drink, its style of life, work and clothing, even customary attitudes, entertainment and art; and it is impossible to order them in a world in which each thing, every single region, receives its due and no one of them obtains too much or too little. With praiseworthy modesty, therefore, he announces that even the general remarks following (p. 92) are only problems (p. 99). They are presented under the following headings. (1) By means of a multitude of causes a common climate is promoted on earth favorable to the existence of living things. (2) The habitable areas of our globe are concentrated in regions where the majority of living things act after the fashion most suitable for them; this disposition of the land masses exercises an influence on their various climates. (3) By virtue of the formation of the earth into mountains, not only was the climate itself endlessly modified for the great majority of living beings, but also the dispersal of the human race was averted, to the extent that it can be averted.

In the fourth section of this Book the author maintains that the genetic force is the mother of all formations on earth which the climate only affects favorably or adversely, and he concludes with some remarks on the conflict between genesis and climate. Among other things he also expresses the wish here for a physico-geographical history dealing with the descent and transformation of our race according to climate and epoch.

In the eighth Book he pursues the problem of the use of the human senses, man's power of imagination, his practical understanding, and his instincts toward happiness, and he illustrates
60   the influence of tradition, opinion, practice, and custom by examples drawn from different peoples.

The ninth Book deals with man's dependence on other men for the development of his faculties, language as the vehicle for human culture, the discovery of the arts and sciences by means of imitation, reason and language, and governments as firmly established systems [which evolved], for the most part,

from inherited traditions. He concludes with remarks on religion and the oldest tradition.[9]

The tenth Book, to a large extent, contains the result of
thoughts that the author has already expounded elsewhere.
Besides remarks on the first habitat of men and Asian traditions concerning the creation of the world and the human
race, it recapitulates the essentials of his hypothesis on the
Mosaic history of creation from his writing, *The Most Ancient
Document of the Human Race.* Our brief résumé of this part
is only meant to be an indication of its contents, not a statement of the spirit of the work. It is intended as an invitation
to read the work, not to replace the reading or render it unnecessary.

Books Six and Seven, for the most part, contain only extracts
from existing ethnic accounts, ably edited, to be sure, master-
fully managed and everywhere accompanied by penetrating
personal judgments; but precisely on that account it is so much
the less capable of a detailed abridgment. It is not our intention here to pick out or analyze any of the bountiful number
of beautiful passages rich in poetic eloquence which will recommend themselves to every reader of feeling. But just briefly
we want to question whether the poetic spirit that enlivens the
expression does not sometimes also intrude into the author's
philosophy; whether synonyms are not valued as definitions
here and there and allegories as truths; whether instead of
occasional neighborly excursions out of the area of the philosophic into the sphere of poetic language the limits and do-
mains of both are not completely disarranged; whether frequently the tissue of daring metaphors, poetic images, and
mythological allusions does not serve to conceal the corpus of
thought as under a farthingale instead of letting it glimmer
forth agreeably as under a translucent veil. We will leave it

9 [The chapter heading in the ninth Book to which Kant refers is:
"Religion is the oldest and holiest tradition on earth." For Herder, therefore, the oldest tradition is religion, not something else that accompanies
it, as Kant suggests here.]

61   to the critics of discriminating philosophic style or to the finish-
ing touch of the author himself to decide, for instance, if it
were not better to say: "not only day and night and the rotation of seasons modify the climate," than what appears on
p. 99: "Not only day and night and the round dance of alter-
nating seasons modify the climate." We will leave it to them
to decide if the following, doubtlessly beautiful image on
p. 100 expressed in a dithyrambic ode is suitably adapted to a
natural historical description of these modifications: "Around
the throne of Jupiter the hours (those of the earth) perform a
round dance, and whatever is formed under their feet only
represents indeed an imperfect perfection because everything
is founded on the fusion of heterogeneous elements; but
through an inner love and communion with one another is
the child of nature—physical regularity and beauty—everywhere
born." Let them decide whether or not the following turn of
expression with which the eighth Book commences is too epic
for the transition from observations made by our describer of
travels on the organization of different peoples and the climate,
to a collection of common propositions deduced therefrom:
"As one who embarks from the waves of the sea upon a voyage
into the air I feel exhilarated since I am coming now, after
having dealt with the forms and natural forces of mankind,
to its spirit and dare to explore its mutable qualities on our
spacious globe using unfamiliar, insufficient, and, in part, uncertain reports." Likewise we will not inquire whether the
stream of his eloquence does not involve him occasionally in
contradictions. On p. 248, for instance, we are told that in-
ventors must often leave more of the profit of their discovery
to posterity than they themselves retain. Does this not exemplify the confirmation of the principle that the natural tendencies of man, which apply to the use of his reason, were
intended to be completely developed only in the species, but
not in the individual? The author is inclined to consider this
principle, p. 206, along with others deriving from it, although
he does not quite grasp them correctly, as almost an offense to
the majesty of nature (which others prosaically call blasphemy).

All of these details we must leave untouched, mindful of the limits which are fixed for us.

There is one thing the reviewer would have wished, not only with regard to our author, but also to any other person engaged in writing a general natural history of humanity, namely, that the way should be prepared by a historically critical mind which would select from the enormous mass of ethnic descriptions or tales of travel, and from all of their accounts which presumably pertain to human nature, principally those which 62 contradict one another, and would have placed them side by side with reminders of the credibility of each author. Then no one would be so audacious as to rely on partial accounts without first having carefully considered the reports of others. But as it is, working with a mass of descriptions dealing with different lands, it is possible to prove, if one cares to do so, that Americans, Tibetans and other genuinely Mongolian tribes have no beards, but also, if one prefers, that they are collectively bearded by nature and only pluck themselves clean. Or one can prove that Americans and Negroes are relatively inferior races in their intellectual capacities, but on the other hand, according to reports just as plausible, that their natural potentialities are on the same level as those of any other inhabitants of the planet. Consequently the philosopher has the option either to admit natural distinctions or to judge everything according to the principle *tout comme chez nous*.[10] But then all of his systems constructed on such a shifting foundation must necessarily assume the appearance of tumble-down hypotheses.

The division of the human species into races does not find favor with our author; he is especially hostile to the classification based on hereditary coloration, probably because he does not yet clearly conceive the notion of race. In number three of Book Seven he calls the cause of the climatic differences among men a genetic force. The reviewer will formulate an idea of the meaning of this expression in the sense intended by the author. On the one hand, he wants to reject the system

[10] ["By our own standards alone."]

of evolution; on the other hand, however, he also wants to reject the purely mechanical influence of external causes as worthless explanations. He admits an inner vital principle which modifies itself according to variations in external conditions and adapts itself to them: this would be the cause of the climatic differences among men. The reviewer would be in full agreement with him but for one reservation: if this cause, organized from within, were limited by its nature only to a certain number and degree of variations in the development of its creatures (thus established it would no longer be free to form another type under changed circumstances), then one could still call this natural function of formative nature seeds or original tendencies, without thereby viewing the variations as buds or machines deposited in the primordial conditions of the world which display themselves only occasionally (as in the system of evolution). Rather they could be viewed simply as limitations—otherwise inexplicable—of a self-constituting faculty acting on itself. These limitations we simply cannot explain further or render comprehensible.

63

A new line of thought begins in the eighth Book which continues to the end of this section and contains the origin of the education of man who is conceived as a rational and moral creature, consequently the commencement of all culture. In the author's opinion this is not to be sought in the power peculiar to the human species, but completely outside it in an understanding of and instruction by other natures. As a result, all progress in culture would only be a projected communication and fortuitous proliferation of an original tradition. It is to this and not to himself that man would have to attribute all of his progress toward wisdom. Since the reviewer, if he sets foot outside of nature and the path that reason offers to knowledge, feels quite helpless, and since he is altogether inexperienced in scholarly philology and the knowledge or critical examination of ancient documents, he is completely incompetent to make philosophic use of the facts that are related and verified in that branch of knowledge. Thus he concedes that he could hold no opinion on this point. At the same time, the copious reading and the special talent of the author to assemble scattered data under one rubric probably allows us to assume in advance at least that we will read many beautiful pages concerning the current of human affairs, which can serve to familiarize us better with the character of the species, and even with certain classical distinctions which can be instructive even for him who might be of a different opinion regarding the first beginning of all human culture. The author very briefly expresses the basis of his own personal opinion (pp. 338-39, including the footnote): "This didactic history (of Moses) relates that the first created men participated in the teaching of Elohim and that with His guidance, through a knowledge of the animals, they acquired language and dominant reason. Since, in a forbidden way, man wanted to become exactly like them in the knowledge of evil, he achieved this to his regret, and from then on, banished, he began a new artificial style of life. If then the Godhead had wanted man to exercise reason and foresight, it would have had to assist him with reason and foresight. . . . But now how has Elohim helped humankind, that is, instructed, advised and informed us? If it is not just as audacious to pose the question as to answer it, we will see elsewhere that tradition itself provides some information on the matter." 64

In an uncharted desert a thinker, like a traveler, must be free to choose his route at discretion. We should attend to how he succeeds; and if, after he has reached his goal, he returns home again to the domicile of reason, safe and sound at the correct hour, he can even anticipate having followers. The reviewer has nothing to say, therefore, concerning the course of thought upon which the author has entered. But the reviewer does believe that he is justified in coming to the defense of some of the propositions attacked by the author in his course of thought because that same freedom cannot be denied him to prescribe a path for himself. In fact, p. 260 reads: "This would be an *easy* principle, to be sure, but a *vicious* one for

a philosophy of the history of mankind: man is an animal who
has need of a master and expects from him, or a union of
them, the felicity of his final destiny."[11] The experience of all
times and all nations may confirm that this principle is ever
easy, but why vicious? We read on p. 205: "Providence considered well in preferring to the artificial ends pursued by great
societies the more pristine felicity of individual men, and
sparing for a time, as far as possible, those expensive machines
of state." Quite right, but first of all the happiness of an animal, then that of a child, then that of youth, and finally the
felicity of a man. In all epochs of mankind, likewise in all
social strata in the same epoch, we find a felicity which is exactly commensurate to the concepts and customs of the creature in the conditions in which it was born and matured.
Indeed, so far as this point is concerned, a comparison of the
degree of happiness and an advantage of one human class or
one generation over another is not even possible. But what if
the true purpose of providence would not be this shadow of
happiness that each man forms for himself, but rather the
endlessly growing and progressing activity and culture which
are thereby brought into play, the apex of which can only be
the product of a state constitution ordered according to the
concepts of human right and, therefore, a work of men themselves? According to p. 206 it would be that "each man has
the measure of his happiness within him," without yielding
anything in the enjoyment of this happiness to any of his suc-
cessors. But so far as the value is concerned—not the value of
their condition when they exist, but the value of existence
itself, that is, why they exist—a wise intention for the existence of any of them would be revealed only in the whole.
Does the author mean that, if the happy inhabitants of Tahiti,
never visited by more civilized nations, were destined to live
in their quiet indolence for thousands of centuries, one could
give a satisfactory answer to the question why they bothered
to exist at all, and whether it would not have been just as

[11] [Cf. "Idea for a Universal History," p. 17 above.]

well that this island should have been occupied by happy sheep and cattle as by happy men engaged in mere pleasure? That principle then is not so vicious as the author thinks. It may well be that a vicious man uttered it.[12]

A second principle to be protected would be this. P. 212 reads: "If someone said that not the individual man but the species could be educated, he would be speaking unintelligibly for me since race and species are only general concepts, except to the extent that they exist in individual beings. . . . As if I could speak of animality, minerality or metality in general and adorned them with the grandest attributes which, however, contradict one another in single individuals! . . . Averroistic philosophy shall not change our philosophy of history in this way." Of course, whoever said that no single horse has horns but the horse species nevertheless is horned would have been uttering a gross absurdity. For species then means nothing more than the characteristic in virtue of which all individuals must directly agree with one another. But if by human species we understand the totality of a series of generations proceeding into infinity (the indeterminable) —and this meaning, after all, is quite common; and if it is admitted that this line of descent ceaselessly approaches its concurrent destination, then it is no contradiction to say that this line is asymptotic in all its parts to this line of destiny, and on the whole, coincides with it. In other words, no single member in all of these generations of the human race, but only the species, fully achieves its destination. The mathematician can offer explanations on this matter. The philosopher would say that the destination of the human race in general is perpetual progress, and its perfection is a simple, but in all respects very useful, Idea of the goal to which, conforming to the purpose of providence, we have to direct our efforts.

Still, this misunderstanding in the passage cited above is only a trifle. More important is its conclusion: "Averroistic

12 [An ironical reference to Kant himself, who defends this principle. Cf. "Idea for a Universal History," p. 16 above.]

philosophy (it says) shall not change our philosophy of history
66 in this way." From this it may be concluded that our author,
so often offended by everything hitherto passed off for philosophy, will now, once and for all in this exhaustive work, give
the world a model of the true art of philosophizing, not in
fruitless verbalisms but in deed and example.

CONJECTURAL BEGINNING OF
HUMAN HISTORY

It is surely permissible to insert here and there conjectures into the progression of an historical account, in order to fill gaps in the record. For what precedes the gaps (the remote cause) and what follows them (the effect) give a fairly reliable clue to the discovery of the intermediate causes, which are to make the transition intelligible. But to *originate* an historical account from conjectures alone would seem to be not much better than to draft a novel. Indeed, this could not be called a conjectural history but rather a mere piece of fiction.

But what may not legitimately be ventured with regard to the progression of the history of human actions may be attempted with regard to their first beginning. At least insofar as this beginning is made by nature, one may attempt to establish it on the basis of pure conjecture. For here one need not resort to fiction but can rely on experience, if only one presupposes that human actions were in the first beginning no better and no worse than we find them now—a presupposition which is according to the analogy of nature and altogether safe. Hence a historical account of the first development of freedom from its original predisposition in human nature is something altogether different from an account of the progression of freedom. For the latter can be based on records alone.

However, conjectures cannot make too high a claim on one's assent. They cannot announce themselves as serious business, but at best only as a permissible exercise of the imagination guided by reason, undertaken for the sake of relaxation and mental health. Hence they are no match for a history which reports the same events as an actually recorded occurrence, and which is accepted as such a report; for the latter is examined by standards quite different from those of mere philosophy of nature. But precisely because of this difference, and because I here venture on a mere pleasure trip, I may hope to be favored with the permission to use, as a map for my trip, a sacred document; and also to fancy that my trip—undertaken on the wings of the imagination, albeit not without a clue rationally derived from experience—may take the very route sketched out in that document. Let the reader consult it (Gen. 2-6) and check at every point whether the road which philosophy takes with the help of concepts coincides with the story told in Holy Writ.

Unless one is to indulge in irresponsible conjectures, one must start out with something which human reason cannot derive from prior natural causes—in the present case, the existence of man. Moreover, it must be man as an adult, because he must get along without the help of a mother; it must be a pair, in order that he may perpetuate his kind; and it must be a single pair. (This is necessary in order that war should not originate at once, what with men being close to each other and yet strangers. Also, if there were an original diversity of descent, nature could be accused of having ignored the most suitable means to bring about the highest end intended for man, namely, sociability [*Geselligkeit*]; for undoubtedly to that end the descent of all men from a single family was the best arrangement.) I put this pair into a place secure against the attack of wild beasts, a place richly endowed by nature with all means of nourishment and blessed with a perpetually mild climate, hence a garden, as it were. What is still more, I begin with this pair, not in the natural state with all its crudeness, but rather after it has already taken mighty steps in the skillful use of its powers. For if I were to attempt to fill this gap—which presumably encompasses a great space of time—there might be for the reader too many conjectures and too few probabilities. The first man, then, was able to stand and walk; he could speak (2:20) [1] and even discourse, i.e., speak according

---

[1] While as yet alone, man must have been moved by the urge for communication to make his existence known to other living beings, particularly to such as utter sounds. These sounds he could imitate, and they could later on serve as names. A similar effect of the above urge may be

to coherent concepts (2:23), and hence think. These are all skills which he had to acquire for himself (for if he were created with them, he would also pass them on through heredity; but this contradicts experience). But I take him as already in **111** possession of these skills. For my sole purpose is to consider the development of manners and morals [*des Sittlichen*] in his way of life, and these already presuppose the skills referred to.

In the beginning, the novice must have been guided by instinct alone, that voice of God which is obeyed by all animals. This permitted some things to be used for nourishment, while forbidding others (3:2, 3). Here it is not necessary to assume a special instinct which is now lost. It could simply have been the sense of smell, plus its affinity with the organ of taste and the well-known relation of the latter to the organs of digestion; in short an ability, perceivable even now, to sense, prior to the consumption of a certain foodstuff, whether or not it is fit for consumption. It is not even necessary to assume that this sensitivity was keener in the first pair than it is now. For it is a familiar enough fact that men wholly absorbed by their senses have much greater perceptive powers than those who, occupied with thoughts as well as with the senses, are to a degree turned away from the sensuous.

So long as inexperienced man obeyed this call of nature all was well with him. But soon reason began to stir. A sense different from that to which instinct was tied—the sense, say, of sight—presented other food than that normally consumed as similar to it; and reason, instituting a comparison, sought to enlarge its knowledge of foodstuffs beyond the bounds of instinctual knowledge (3:6). This experiment might, with good luck, have ended well, even though instinct did not advise it, so long as it was at least not contrary to instinct. But reason

---

observed even now. Children and thoughtless persons are apt to disturb the thinking part of the community by rattling, shouting, whistling, singing and other kinds of noisy entertainment, often also by religious devotions of such a nature. I can see no motive for such conduct except the wish on the part of those who engage in it to make their existence known to one and all.

has this peculiarity that, aided by the imagination, it can create artificial desires which are not only unsupported by natural instinct but actually contrary to it. These desires, in the beginning called concupiscence, gradually generate a whole host of unnecessary and indeed unnatural inclinations called luxuriousness. The original occasion for deserting natural instinct may have been trifling. But this was man's first attempt to become conscious of his reason as a power which can extend itself beyond the limits to which all animals are confined. As such its effect was very important and indeed decisive for his future way of life. Thus the occasion may have been merely the external appearance of a fruit which tempted because of its similarity to tasty fruits of which man had already partaken. In addition there may have been the example of an animal which consumed it because, for it, it was naturally fit for consumption, while on the contrary, being harmful for man, it was consequently resisted by man's instinct. Even so, this was a sufficient occasion for reason to do violence to the voice of nature (3:1) and, its protest notwithstanding, to make the first attempt at a free choice; an attempt which, being the first, probably did not have the expected result. But however insignificant the damage done, it sufficed to open man's eyes (3:7). He discovered in himself a power of choosing for himself a way of life, of not being bound without alternative to a single way, like the animals. Perhaps the discovery of this advantage created a moment of delight. But of necessity, anxiety and alarm as to how he was to deal with this newly discovered power quickly followed; for man was a being who did not yet know either the secret properties or the remote effects of anything. He stood, as it were, at the brink of an abyss. Until that moment instinct had directed him toward specific objects of desire. But from these there now opened up an infinity of such objects, and he did not yet know how to choose between them. On the other hand, it was impossible for him to return to the state of servitude (i.e., subjection to instinct) from the state of freedom, once he had tasted the latter.

Next to the instinct for food, by means of which nature preserves the individual, the greatest prominence belongs to the sexual instinct, by means of which she preserves the species. Reason, once aroused, did not delay in demonstrating its influence here as well. In the case of animals, sexual attraction is merely a matter of transient, mostly periodic impulse. But man soon discovered that for him this attraction can be prolonged and even increased by means of the imagination—a power which carries on its business, to be sure, the more moderately, but at once also the more constantly and uniformly, the more its object is removed from the senses. By means of the imagination, he discovered, the surfeit was avoided which goes with the satisfaction of mere animal desire. The fig leaf (3:7), then, 113 was a far greater manifestation of reason than that shown in the earlier stage of development. For the one shows merely a power to choose the extent to which to serve impulse; but the other—rendering an inclination more inward [*inniglich*] and constant by removing its object from the senses—already reflects consciousness of a certain degree of mastery of reason over impulse. *Refusal* was the feat which brought about the passage from merely sensual [*empfundenen*] to spiritual [*idealischen*] attractions, from mere animal desire gradually to love, and along with this from the feeling of the merely agreeable to a taste for beauty, at first only for beauty in man but at length for beauty in nature as well. In addition, there came a first hint at the development of man as a moral creature. This came from the sense of decency [*Sittsamkeit*], which is an inclination to inspire others to respect by proper manners, i.e., by concealing all that which might arouse low esteem. Here, incidentally, lies the real basis of all true sociability [*Geselligkeit*].

This may be a small beginning. But if it gives a wholly new direction to thought, such a beginning is epoch-making. It is then more important than the whole immeasurable series of expansions of culture which subsequently spring from it.

After having thus insinuated itself into the first immediately felt needs, reason took its third step. This was the conscious *expectation of the future*. This capacity for facing up in the

present to the often very distant future, instead of being wholly
absorbed by the enjoyment of the present, is the most decisive
mark of the human's advantage. It enables man to prepare
himself for distant aims according to his role as a human being. But at the same time it is also the most inexhaustible
source of cares and troubles, aroused by the uncertainty of his
future—cares and troubles of which animals are altogether free
(3:13-19). Man, compelled to support himself, his wife and his
future children, foresaw the ever-increasing hardships of labor.
Woman foresaw the troubles to which nature had subjected
her sex, and those additional ones to which man, a being
stronger than she, would subject her. Both foresaw with fear
—in the background of the picture and at the end of a troublesome life—that which, to be sure, inexorably strikes all animals without, however, causing them care, namely, death. And
they apparently foreswore and decried as a crime the use of
reason, which had been the cause of all these ills. Perhaps their
sole comfort was the prospect of living through their children
114 who might enjoy a better fortune, or else the hope that these
latter members of their family might alleviate their burden
(3:16-20).

But there was yet a fourth and final step which reason took,
and this raised man altogether above community with animals.
He came to understand, however obscurely, that he is the true
end of nature, and that nothing that lives on earth can compete with him in this regard. The first time he ever said to
the sheep, "nature has given you the skin you wear for my use,
not for yours"; the first time he ever took that skin and put
it upon himself (3:21)—that time he became aware of the way
in which his nature privileged and raised him above all animals. And from then on he looked upon them, no longer
as fellow creatures, but as mere means and tools to whatever
ends he pleased. This idea entails (obscurely, to be sure) the
idea of contrast, that what he may say to an animal he may
not say to a fellow human; that he must rather consider the
latter as an equal participant in the gifts of nature. This idea
was the first preparation of all those restraints in his relations
with his fellow men which reason would in due course impose

on man's will, restraints which are far more essential for the establishment of a civil society than inclination and love.

Thus man had entered into a relation of equality with all rational beings, whatever their rank (3:22), with respect to the claim of being an end in himself, respected as such by everyone, a being which no one might treat as a mere means to ulterior ends. So far as natural gifts are concerned, other beings may surpass man beyond all comparison. Nevertheless, man is without qualification equal even to higher beings in that none has the right to use him according to pleasure. This is because of his reason—reason considered not insofar as it is a tool to the satisfaction of his inclinations, but insofar as it makes him an end in himself. Hence this last step of reason is at the same time man's *release* from the womb of nature, an alteration of condition which is honorable, to be sure, but also fraught with danger. For nature had now driven him from the safe and harmless state of childhood—a garden, as it were, which looked after his needs without any trouble on his part (3:23)—into the wide world, where so many cares, troubles, and unforeseen ills awaited him. In the future, the wretchedness of his condition would often arouse in him the wish for a paradise, the creation of his imagination, where he could dream or while away his existence in quiet inactivity and permanent peace. But between 115 him and that imagined place of bliss, restless reason would interpose itself, irresistibly impelling him to develop the faculties implanted within him. It would not permit him to return to that crude and simple state from which it had driven him to begin with (3:24). It would make him take up patiently the toil which he yet hates, and pursue the frippery which he despises. It would make him forget even death itself which he dreads, because of all those trifles which he is even more afraid to lose.

Remark

From this account of original human history we may conclude: man's departure from that paradise which his reason represents as the first abode of his species was nothing but the transition from an uncultured, merely animal condition to the state of humanity, from bondage to instinct to rational control—in a word, from the tutelage of nature to the state of freedom. Whether man has won or lost in this change is no longer an open question, if one considers the destiny of his species. This consists in nothing less than progress toward perfection, be the first attempts toward that aim, or even the first long series of attempts, ever so faulty.

However, while for the species the direction of this road may be from worse to better, this is not true for the individual. Before reason awoke, there was as yet neither commandment nor prohibition and hence also no violation of either. But when reason began to set about its business, it came, in all its pristine weakness, into conflict with animality, with all its power. Inevitably evils sprang up, and (which is worse) along with the cultivation of reason also vices, such as had been wholly alien to the state of ignorance and innocence. Morally, the first step from this latter state was therefore a fall; physically, it was a punishment, for a whole host of formerly unknown ills were a consequence of this fall. The history of nature therefore begins with good, for it is the work of God, while the history of freedom begins with wickedness, for it is the work of man. For the individual, who in the use of his freedom is concerned only with himself, this whole change was a loss; for nature, whose purpose with man concerns the species, it was a gain. Hence the individual must consider as his own fault, not only every act of wickedness which he commits, but also all the evils which he suffers; and yet at the same time, insofar as he is a member of a whole (a species), he must admire and praise the wisdom and purposiveness of the whole arrangement.

In this way it is possible to reconcile, both with reason and with each other, the assertions of the celebrated J. J. Rousseau. These are often misinterpreted and do, indeed, have an appearance of inconsistency. In his *On the Influence of the Sciences* and his *On the Inequality of Man* he shows quite correctly that there is an inevitable conflict between culture and the human species, considered as a natural species of which every member ought wholly to attain his natural end. But in his *Émile,* his *Social Contract,* and other writings he tries to solve this much harder problem: how culture was to move forward, in order to bring about such a development of the dispositions of mankind, considered as a *moral* species, as to end the conflict between the natural and the moral species. Now here it must be seen that all evils which express human life, and all vices which dishonor it, spring from this unresolved conflict.[2] This conflict is in fact altogether unresolved,

[2] I will mention the following, by way of giving a few examples of this conflict between man's striving toward the fulfillment of his moral destiny, on the one hand, and, on the other, his unalterable subjection to laws fit for the uncivilized and animal state.

When he is about sixteen or seventeen years old, nature makes man come of age; that is, she gives him both the desire and the power to reproduce his kind. In the uncivilized state of nature, a youth literally becomes a man at that age. He is then able to look after himself, to reproduce his kind, and to take care of both a wife and children. This is easy because his needs are simple. But in order to discharge the responsibilities of manhood in the civilized state, one needs means and skills, as well as fortunate external circumstances. Hence a youth acquires the civil aspect of manhood on the average only about ten years later. But as society increases in complexity nature does not alter the age of sexual maturity. She stubbornly perseveres in her law, which aims at the perpetuation of man as an animal species. Hence manners and morals, and the aim of nature, inevitably come to interfere with each other. For as a natural being a person is already a man at an age when as a civil being (who yet does not cease to be a natural being as well) he is still a youth or even a child. For thus one may well call a person unable, in the civil state, to provide for himself, let alone for others of his kind. Yet he has the urge and capacity to reproduce his kind. What is more, he also has the nature-given vocation to do so. For surely nature has not endowed living beings with instincts and capacities in order that they should fight and suppress them. The disposition in question, then, did not intend the civilized state, but merely the preservation of man as an animal species. And the civilized state comes into inevitable conflict with that disposition. This conflict only a perfect civil constitution could end, and indeed such a constitution is the ultimate end at which all culture aims. But the space of time during which there is still conflict is as a rule filled with vices and their consequences—the various kinds of human misery.

This, then, is one example to prove that nature has given us two different dispositions for two different purposes, the one for man as an

because culture, considered as the genuine education of man
as man and citizen, has perhaps not even begun properly,
117   much less been completed. Sometimes a natural impulse toward vice is mistakenly identified as the ultimate cause of these
evils. But in itself and as a natural disposition, impulse serves
a good purpose. The real trouble is that, on the one hand, culture progressively interferes with its natural function, by
altering the conditions to which it was suited; while on the
other hand, natural impulse interferes with culture until such

---

animal, the other for him as a moral species. Another example is the *ars
longa, vita brevis* of Hippocrates.* A single man of talent, who had
reached mature judgment through long practice and acquisition of knowledge, could further the arts and sciences far more than whole generations
of scholars, if only he could live, mentally alert, for the length of their
life-spans added together. But nature has apparently disposed concerning
the length of human life with ends other than the furtherance of the sciences in view. For just when the luckiest of thinkers is on the verge of
the greatest discoveries which his trained intellect and experience entitle
him to hope for, just then old age sets in. His mind becomes dull, and
he must leave to another generation the task of adding a step in the
progress of culture; and that generation must once more begin with the
ABC, and once more travel the whole road which that thinker had already traversed. Hence the road of the human species toward its destined
goal appears to be subject to ceaseless interruptions, and mankind in perpetual danger of lapsing into ancient savagery. Not entirely without reason does the Greek philosopher complain: it is a pity that one must die
when one has just begun to learn how one should have lived.

Human inequality may serve as our third example, not inequality as
regards natural talent or worldly good fortune, but with regard to universal human rights. There is much truth in Rousseau's complaint about
118   this inequality. At the same time, it is inseparable from culture, so long
as the latter progresses without plan, as it were; and this too is for a
long time inevitable. Surely nature did not intend this inequality, for she
gave man freedom and along with it reason, by which to limit this freedom through nothing other than its own inherent conformity to law, a
universal and external lawfulness which is called *civil right*. Man was
meant to rise by his own labors above the crudeness of his natural dispositions, and yet in so doing to take care lest he do violence to them.
But he can expect to acquire the skill for this only at a late date and
after many abortive attempts. In the meantime, mankind groans under
the burden of evils which, in its inexperience, it inflicts on itself.

   * ["Art is long, life is short" (*Aphorisms* I. 1).]

time as finally art will be strong and perfect enough to become a second nature. This indeed is the ultimate moral end of the human species.

THE END OF HISTORY

The following period began with man's passage from an age of comfort and peace to one of labor and strife. This latter was the prelude of unification through society. We place man into a condition in which he owned tame animals, as well as crops for nourishment, which he himself could produce by sowing and planting (4:2). To place him in this condition requires of us, once again, a big leap. For in actual fact the transition from the existence of a wild huntsman to that of a keeper of tame animals, and from haphazard digging for roots or fruit-gathering to an agricultural way of life must have been slow enough. Until that time men had lived peacefully side by side. But here that strife had to begin which separated those of a different way of life, and dispersed men all over the earth. The existence of the herdsman is not only leisurely, it is also economically the safest; for there is no shortage of grazing land in sparsely populated country. But agriculture is troublesome, dependent on the caprices of climate, and hence insecure. Moreover, the farmer needs a permanent habitation, land of his own, and sufficient power to protect it. But because it limits his freedom of pasture, the herdsman hates the farmer's property. Because of their difference in condition, the farmer could seem to envy the herdsman, and regard him as more favored by heaven (4:4). In fact, however, he rather considered him a nuisance, so long as he remained in his neighborhood. For graz- 119 ing cattle do not spare the crops. Now the herdsman, having done his damage, can always take his cattle and go elsewhere, escaping all responsibility. This is easy for him, for he leaves nothing behind which he would not find elsewhere. Hence it was probably the farmer who first resorted to force in order to end the nuisance which the other had created. The latter probably was conscious of no wrongdoing. And it was probably the farmer who finally removed himself as far as possible from those who lived the life of the herdsman. For in no other way would the encroachments, or at least the danger that he might lose the fruits of his long, industrious labor, ever wholly cease. This separation inaugurated the third epoch.

Where sustenance depends on the cultivation of the soil—especially the planting of trees—there is need for permanent housing. This in turn the inhabitants must be able to defend against attacks; and in order to be able to do so they must be organized to assist each other. Given such a way of life, then, men could no longer live isolated, in small families. They had to band together and build villages (improperly called towns). Only thus could they protect their property against the attacks of wild hunters or bands of roving herdsmen. It now first became possible to acquire by mutual exchange those basic necessities of life which had been made into necessities by an altered way of life (4:20). This was bound to give rise to the first beginnings of culture, of art, of entertainment and of the habit of industriousness (4:21, 22). But above all it had to give rise to some kind of civil order and public administration of justice. Such administration, to be sure, at first concerned itself only with the most flagrant acts of violence. These were no longer to be avenged by individuals, as had been the case in the savage state. They were to be punished by an authority, which acted according to law and which was the highest power. This authority preserved the unity of the whole and was a kind of government (4:23, 24).

From this crude original disposition all human skills could gradually develop, skills of which that of sociability and securing public safety is the most beneficial. The human species could multiply. It could spread from a center, like a beehive, sending everywhere as colonists men already civilized. With this epoch, too, human inequality began, that rich source of so many evils but also of everything good. Later on, inequality increased.

The nomadic people recognize God alone as their Lord. The
city dwellers and farmers, on the other hand, have a human

master in the form of government (6:4).[3] Because of its opposition to land-ownership, the former group feels ill will to the latter two, and is hated by them in turn. Hence so long as the one surrounds the other two there is continuous warfare between them, or at least continuous danger of war. But both sides can at least rejoice in the priceless possession of liberty. (Even now, the danger of war is the only factor which mitigates despotism. For a state cannot be powerful unless it is wealthy, but without liberty, wealth-producing activities cannot flourish. This is why a poor nation requires the broad support of a citizenry intensely committed to its survival, to take the place of its lack of wealth. But such support, again, is possible only in a free nation.) Nevertheless, it is inevitable that the herdsmen should increasingly be tempted to establish relations with the city dwellers, and to let themselves be drawn into the glittering misery of their cities (6:2). The temptation consists in the incipient luxury of the cities, manifest especially in the art of charming by which the city women came to show up the slatternly wenches of the desert. Now on the one hand this fusion of two formerly hostile groups ends the danger of war. But on the other it is also the end of all liberty. The result is a despotism of powerful tyrants and—culture having barely begun—not only an abominable state of slavery, but along with it soulless sense-indulgence mixed with all the vices of an as yet uncivilized condition. A further result is also that the human species is irresistibly turned away from the task assigned to it by nature, the progressive cultivation of its disposition to goodness. Thus the human species became unworthy of its destiny, which is not to live in brutish pleasure or slavish servitude, but to rule over the earth (6:17).

[3] The Arab Bedouins even now call themselves children of a former sheik, the founder of their tribe (e.g., Beni Haled). But their sheik is by no means their master, and he cannot rule over them according to his pleasure. For in a nomadic people nobody owns real estate which he would have to leave behind if he went away. Hence a family which does not like the way its tribe is run can simply leave it, and strengthen another by joining it.

Concluding Remark

A thoughtful person is acquainted with a kind of distress
which threatens his moral fibre, a kind of distress of which the
thoughtless know nothing: discontent with Providence which
121 governs the course of this world. This distress he is apt to
feel when he considers the evils which oppress the human
species so heavily and, apparently, so hopelessly. It is true that
Providence has assigned to us a toilsome road on earth. But it
is of the utmost importance that we should nevertheless be
content, partly in order that we may gather courage even in
the midst of toils, partly in order that we should not lose sight
of our own failings. These are perhaps the sole cause of all the
evils which befall us, and we might seek help against them by
improving ourselves. But this we should fail to do if we blamed
all these evils on fate.

Undoubtedly war is the greatest source of the evils which oppress civilized nations; not so much actual war, but rather
the never-ceasing and indeed ever-increasing preparation for a
future war. All the resources of the state are used to this end,
as well as all the fruits of its culture, which might instead be
used for the creation of a still greater culture. In many places
freedom is curtailed because of war, and the motherly care of
the state for its individual members turns into unrelenting and
harsh demands, a harshness which is justified because of dangers threatening from abroad. All this must be admitted. And
yet, were it not for this perpetual fear of war, would there be
the culture which in fact exists? Would there be a close coalition between social classes, brought about for mutual economic
benefit? Would there be such large populations? Would there
be even as much freedom as does, after all, remain, albeit
under laws which greatly restrict it? For it is surely the fear of
war which extorts from the heads of state at least this much respect for humanity. One need but think of China which, because of its geographical situation, has to fear at most the
odd, unforeseen small attack, but no powerful enemy; and
where for that reason every trace of freedom is extinct.

In the present state of human culture, then, war is an indispensable means to the still further development of human culture. Only in a state of perfect culture would perpetual peace be of benefit to us, and only then would it be possible. But God alone knows when this will be achieved. With respect to war, then, we are surely ourselves the cause of the evils which we lament so bitterly. And Holy Writ is quite right in regarding the fusion of peoples into one society—and their complete liberation from external dangers at a time when their culture had hardly begun—as an impediment to all further cultural progress, and a plunge into incurable corruption.

The second cause of human dissatisfaction with the order of 122 nature is the shortness of life. To be sure, a man who can wish that life should last longer than in fact it does must be a poor judge of its value. Its greater length would merely prolong a game of unceasing war with troubles. But one cannot find fault with those of childish judgment who have no love of life and yet fear death, for whom it is a daily struggle to finish the day in the barest form of contentment, and who still have never enough days to repeat the wretched business. Nevertheless, one need but consider how many cares vex us in our efforts to provide the means for even so short a life, how much injustice is done in the hope of even so short a future enjoyment. And one must reasonably believe that, if men could look forward to a life of 800 or more years, father would have to fear for his life from son, brother from brother, and friend from friend; that the vices of a human species endowed with so long a life would reach a degree where it would deserve no better fate than to be wiped from the face of the earth by a universal flood (6:12, 13).

The third wish is an empty yearning rather than a genuine wish, for those who have it know that its object is forever beyond human reach. This is a golden age, an image so highly praised by poets. In that age we are to be rid of all those imagined needs which voluptuousness now imposes on us. There is to be contentment with the mere satisfaction of natural needs, universal human equality and perpetual peace: in a word, unalloyed enjoyment of a carefree life, dreamt away idly, or trifled away in childish play. Such yearnings have been stimulated by stories such as *Robinson Crusoe* and reports of visitors to the South Sea Islands. The existence of such yearnings proves that thoughtful persons weary of civilized life, if they seek its value in pleasure alone, and if, reminded by reason that they might give value to life by actions, fall back on laziness, to counteract this reminder. But this wish for a return to an age of simplicity and innocence is futile. The foregoing presentation of man's original state teaches us that, because he could not be satisfied with it, man could not remain in this state, much less be inclined ever to return to it; that therefore he must, after all, ascribe his present troublesome condition to himself and his own choice.

An exposition of his history such as the above, then, is useful for man, and conducive to his instruction and improvement. It teaches him that he must not blame the evils which oppress him on Providence, nor attribute his own offense to an original sin committed by his first parents. (For free actions can in no aspects be hereditary.) Such an exposition teaches man that, under like circumstances, he would act exactly like his first parents, that is, abuse reason in the very first use of reason, the advice of nature to the contrary notwithstanding. Hence he must recognize what they have done as his own act, and thus blame only himself for the evils which spring from the abuse of reason. Once the blame for moral evils is correctly laid where it belongs, the strictly physical evils will hardly add up, in the ledger of merit and guilt, to a balance which is in our favor.

This, then, is the lesson taught by a philosophical attempt to write the most ancient part of human history: contentment with Providence, and with the course of human affairs, considered as a whole. For this course is not a decline from good to evil, but rather a gradual development from the worse to the better; and nature itself has given the vocation to everyone to contribute as much to this progress as may be within his power.

123

THE END OF ALL THINGS

It is a common expression, particularly in pious talk, to have a dying person say he is *passing from time into eternity.*

In point of fact, this expression would mean nothing if eternity were to be understood here in the sense of time progressing into infinity; for then surely man would never emerge from time, but would always be merely moving forward from one point in it to another. An *end to all time,* therefore, must be meant by this expression in reference to the uninterrupted duration of man; but this longevity (his existence considered as a quantity), nevertheless, must also mean a quantity (*duratio noumenon*) completely incomparable with the temporal, a notion of which we certainly can form no concept—except, perhaps, a purely negative one. There is something appalling in this thought because it leads, as it were, to the brink of an abyss, and for him who sinks into it, no return is possible. ("Eternity in its mighty embrace / holds fast in that stern place / him who leaves nothing behind," Haller.) [1] And yet there is something alluring in it: for people cannot resist turning their frightened gaze ever anew toward eternity (*nequeunt expleri corda tuendo,* Virgil).[2] The thought is sublime in its terror, partly on account of its obscurity, in which the imagination is usually more powerfully active than in clear light. And, ultimately, it is even required to be interwoven in a wondrous way with common human reason, because this notion of eternity is encountered in all reasoning peoples in all times, garbed in one style or another. While we now follow up the

[1] [Albrecht von Haller (1708-1777), *Unvollkommenes Gedicht über die Ewigkeit* (1736).]

[2] ["Men cannot sate their hearts with gazing on the terrible eyes . . ." (Virgil, *Aeneid* VIII. 265, trans. H. R. Fairclough, "Loeb Classical Library" edn.).]

transition from time to eternity (this idea may or may not have some objective reality regarded theoretically as an enlargement of knowledge), as reason itself makes this transition in a moral respect, we encounter the end of all things considered as beings in time and as objects of possible experience. But this end, in the moral order of purposes, is simultaneously the beginning of a duration of these self-same beings as supersensible, i.e., as not standing under the conditions of time. Consequently, this duration and its status will be susceptible of no other definition of its nature than a moral one.

328   Days are, as it were, the children of time, because each day with all that it contains is the product of the one preceding it. Now just as the last child of its parents is called the youngest child, so our language has chosen to refer to the Last Day (the moment which terminates all time) as the *Youngest Day*.[3] The Last Day, therefore, belongs as yet to time, for something still happens on it (not relevant to eternity where nothing happens, since the passage of time would not pertain to it), namely, the reckoning of men's accounts on the basis of their conduct during their entire life span. It is a *Judgment Day*; the decision of the World-Judge in favor of salvation or damnation is, therefore, the proper end of all things in time and the beginning of (blissful or miserable) eternity in which the fate that has fallen to each man endures as it was allotted to him in the moment of its pronouncement (i.e., of his sentencing). Thus the Last Day also comprehends the Final Judgment. If now there should be counted among the last things the creation of a new heaven and earth for the habitation of the blessed and a hell for the dammed, and not just the end of the world as it appears in its present form—the falling of the stars from the vault of the sky and the collapse of the vault itself (or its disappearance, like a scroll that is rolled up [4]) and the conflagration of both—then that Judgment Day would certainly not be the

3 [*jüngster Tag*. The translation of this sentence is literal; but since the usage Kant appeals to in German does not exist in English, henceforth *jüngster Tag* will be translated as "Last Day."]
4 [An allusion to Rev. 6:14.]

Last Day, for other days would succeed it. But since the idea of an end of all things does not originate from reasoning about physical things but from reasoning about the moral course of the world and nothing else, the moral course of events can be applied only to the supersensible (which is comprehensible only in relation to the moral). The same is true of the idea of eternity. Thus the representation of those last things which are said to come *after* Doomsday, must only be regarded as making Doomsday and its moral consequences, which are not theoretically conceivable to us, in some way perceptible to us.

It is to be noted, however, that from the very earliest ages there have been two systems concerning the coming eternity. One of them, that of the Unitarians, awards salvation to all men (who are purified by means of more or less lengthy penances); the other, that of the Dualists,[5] awards salvation to some select ones, but to all the rest eternal damnation. For a system, according to which all beings would be destined to be damned, could probably not be tenable since thereunder there would be no justification for their having been created in the first place. And, too, the destruction of all beings would signify an imperfect wisdom which, dissatisfied with its own work, knows no other means to remedy its defects except to destroy it. However, precisely the same difficulty always stands in the path of the Dualists that prevents us from contemplating an eternal

329

[5] Such a system in the ancient Persian religion (of Zoroaster) was based on the supposition of two primeval beings, the good principle Ormuzd, and the evil one, Ahriman, engaged in an eternal battle with one another. —It is odd that the language of two lands which are widely removed from each other, but still more so from the present province of the German language, in the denomination of both of these primeval beings, is German. I recall having read in Sonnerat * that in Ava (the land of the Burmese) the good principle is called Godeman (which word also seems to appear in the name *Darius Godomannus*); and since the word Ahriman sounds very much like *arrant* man [*arge Mann*], present-day Persian also contains a large number of originally German words. So it might be a task for the scholar of antiquity, using the clue of *linguistic* relationship, to trace the origins of the current concepts of religion of many peoples. (See Sonnerat's *Travels*, IV, Bk. 2, chap. 2, B).

* [Pierre Sonnerat (1749-1814), author of travelogs to the orient.]

damnation for all men; for it could be asked why even the few
were created, why even a single person alone if he were only
meant to exist in order to be eternally rejected, a thing more
distressing even than not to exist at all.

So far as we can see it, so far as we are able to investigate it
ourselves, the Dualistic system indeed possesses (but only under
one supremely good original being) a preponderance in the
practical sense for every man as he has to judge himself (although not as he is empowered to judge others). For so far as
he knows himself, reason leaves him no other remaining expectation of entering eternity except that which, based on the
conduct he has hitherto shown, his own conscience reveals to
him at the end of his life. But to fashion therefrom a dogma,
that is, a theoretical proposition that is intrinsically (objectively) valid, a simple judgment of reason is far from adequate.
For what person knows himself and others so thoroughly as to
decide whether, in the all-seeing eye of a Judge of the world,
one man has an advantage in every respect over another in
his inner moral worth, if he separates from the causes of his
presumably well-conducted life everything which is called the
wages of success, for example, his congenitally amiable tem-
perament, the naturally greater vigor of his higher powers (of
his understanding and reason so as to check his impulses), and
330 the occasion when chance spared him many temptations which
befall others? And if he does separate all this from his true
character (as he necessarily must subtract it in order to evaluate this thing properly, since he cannot credit it as being a
fortunate gift of his own merit), who will then decide, I say,
whether one man has the advantage of more moral worth over
another? And may it not be perhaps as stupid a self-conceit in
this superficial self-knowledge to pass any judgment in his own
favor concerning his own moral worth (and deserved fate) as
it would be to pass any judgment on others? Consequently the
system of the Unitarian, as well as that of the Dualist, both
considered as dogma, seem totally to exceed the speculative
faculty of human reason, and everything seems to reduce us to
restricting those rational Ideas simply to the conditions of

practical use only. For we still see nothing ahead of us that could apprise us at the present time of our fate in a coming world except the judgment of our own conscience, that is, what our current moral state, so far as we are cognizant of it, permits us rationally to judge of the matter. That is to say, we must judge that those principles of our behavior in life which we have found governing in us (be they good or evil) until its end, will also continue to prevail after death, and we have not the slightest reason to assume an alteration of them in that future. Therefore, we would also have to anticipate consequences commensurate with this fault or that virtue for all eternity under the dominion of the good or evil principle; in this sense it is wise then to so act *as if* another life, and the moral state in which we terminate the present one along with its consequences upon entering the other one, are unchangeable. From a practical point of view, therefore, the system to be embraced will have to be the Dualistic one, especially since the Unitarian system seems to be too much lulled asleep in complacent security; still we do not want to determine which of the two merits preference in a theoretical and purely speculative sense.

But why do people expect an end of the world at all? And even if this is granted them, why precisely a terrifying end (which is the case for the majority of the human race)? The basis for the first belief seems to be that reason tells them the duration of the world has a value only to the extent that ra- 331 tional creatures in it are commensurate with the ultimate purpose of its existence; but if this was not meant to be achieved, creation itself appears to be pointless to them, like a drama that is totally without issue and has no rational design. The second belief is based on the notion of the depraved nature of the human race,[6] which is vast to the point of despair, a race

[6] In all times obscurantist sages (or philosophers), without paying any attention to the natural tendency in human nature toward the good, have exhausted themselves in inimical, partly nauseous, allegories in order to present our world, the domicile of mankind, completely contemptuously: (1) as an *inn* (caravansary), as some dervish regards it, where every man

for which the preparation of an end—and, indeed, a frightful
end—is the only measure proper to the highest wisdom and
justice (in the opinion of the greatest number of people).
Hence the omens of Doomsday also are all of a dreadful kind
(for when is an imagination, excited by great expectation,
wanting in omens and miracles?). Some see them in spreading
injustice, oppression of the poor through the wanton debauch-
ery of the rich, and in the general loss of honesty and faith, or
in the cruel wars which erupt in every corner of the world, etc.;
in a word, people perceive them in moral decay and the rapid
increase of vices along with their accompanying evils, of such
kind, as they fancy, former ages never saw. Others, in comparison, see omens in extraordinary changes in nature, in
earthquakes, storms and floods, or comets and atmospheric
signs.

In point of fact, men, not without reason, feel the burden
of their existence even though they themselves are the cause

---

putting up there along his journey through life must be prepared to be
soon supplanted by a successor; (2) as a *penitentiary*, an opinion for which
the Brahmanic, Tibetan and other Oriental wise men (likewise even Plato)
have a strong affection—a place for the chastisement and purification of
fallen spirits expelled from heaven which are now human or animal
souls; (3) as a *lunatic asylum*, where not only each man destroys his own
aims for himself, but rather one man causes the other all manner of deep
sorrows, and above all, considers it the greatest honor to be able to exercise
his skill and might; finally, (4) as a *cloaca* to which all refuse from other
worlds has been conjured. This last conceit is in a certain sense original
and we owe it to a would-be Persian wit who transplanted paradise, the
abode of the first human couple, to heaven. In this garden, many trees
were to be encountered amply provided with magnificent fruit, the re-
siduum of which, however, disappeared in an imperceptible effluvium
after their enjoyment. An exception was a single tree in the middle of the
garden which bore delicious enough fruit, but of such a kind that did
not allow itself to be so eliminated. Our first parents now longed to taste
its fruit, heedless, however, of the prohibition that they not befoul heaven
with it; there was no relief other than that one of the angels pointed
out to them the far-distant earth with the words, "That is the privy for
the whole universe," then led them thither in order to relieve nature, and,
leaving them behind, flew back to heaven. Now it is from this that the
human race is supposed to have originated on earth.

of it. The reason for this seems to me to lie in the fact that in the progress of the human race the cultivation of talents, art, and taste (with their consequence, luxury) naturally precedes the development of morality; and this situation is precisely the most burdensome and hazardous for morality, as well as for physical weal, because needs increase much more vigorously than the means to satisfy them. But the moral predisposition of mankind which (like Horace's *poena, pede claudo*) [7] always hobbles behind the cultivation of talents will someday overtake it (as one, under a wise world ruler, may well hope), though often stumbling and entangled as it is in its own hasty career. And so considering the empirical proofs for the superiority of morality in our age over all former ages, people themselves perhaps should be able to nourish the hope that the Last Day might rather make its appearance with an Elijah's ascension and bring about the end of all things on earth, than with a descent into hell akin to that of Korah's band. [8] But this heroic faith in virtue seems, after all, not to have so universally vigorous an influence on the conversion of souls as a revelatory scene attended by terrors which is thought of as preceding the last things.

Note. We are dealing (or playing) here simply with Ideas which reason itself creates, the objects of which (if it possesses

[7] [The passage to which Kant is referring reads, *raro antecedentem scelestum deseruit pede Poena claudo:* "but rarely does Vengeance, albeit of halting gait, fail to o'ertake the guilty, though he gain the start" (Horace, *Odes* III. 2. 32, trans. C. E. Bennett, "Loeb Classical Library" edn.).]

[8] ["And it came to pass, as they still went on, and talked, that, behold, there appeared a chariot of fire, and horses of fire, and parted them both asunder; and Elijah went up by a whirlwind into heaven." Kings 2:11.

Korah, at the head of 250 men, led a revolt against Moses, "and the earth opened her mouth and swallowed them up, and their houses, and all the men that appertained unto Korah, and all their goods." Num. 16:32. Strictly speaking, therefore, Kant is incorrect to call Korah's destruction a "descent into hell" (*Höllenfahrt*). The concept of hell was not incorporated into Judaism until the Hellenistic period, and Numbers was conceived and written for the most part in the century following the end of the Exile (536 B.C.).]

any) lie completely beyond our field of vision; [9] and although these Ideas are transcendent for our speculative cognition, they are still not on that account to be considered void in all respects. Made available to us by the legislative reason itself, these Ideas are to be regarded rather in a practical sense, not laboriously pondered with respect to their objects, whatever these are in and of themselves and according to their nature, but rather as we are required to contemplate them on behalf of the moral principles which pertain to the ultimate purpose of all things. (In this way Ideas, which would otherwise be altogether empty, acquire objective practical reality.) And since we are dealing with such Ideas, we have an open field before us to arrange this product of our own reason, the universal concept of an end of all things, according to the relation it bears to our cognitive faculty, and to classify its derivatives.

Accordingly, the whole will be divided and presented in three sections: (1) in the *natural* [10] end of all things conforming to the order of moral ends of divine wisdom which we can, therefore, certainly comprehend (in a practical sense); (2) in its *mystic* (supernatural) end in the order of efficient causes of which we comprehend nothing; (3) in the *unnatural* (perverted) end of all things for which we ourselves are responsible in that we *misunderstand* the ultimate purpose. The first of these possibilities has just been discussed and now the two remaining ones will follow.

In the Apocalypse ([i.e., Revelations] 10:5, 6), "An angel lifted up his hand to heaven, And sware by him that liveth forever and ever, who created heaven, etc.: that there should be time no longer." If one does not assume that this angel

---

[9] [Cf. Introduction, p. xix and note 15.]

[10] *Natural (formaliter)* means that which necessarily proceeds according to laws of a certain order, whatever order that may be, thus even the moral order (therefore, not always merely the physical). Opposed to it is the *non-natural* which can either be the supernatural or the unnatural. The necessary issue from *natural causes* likewise should be presented as materially natural (physically necessary).

"with his voice of seven thunders" (v. 3) [11] desired to cry out nonsense, then he must have meant with these words that henceforth there should be no *change;* for if there were still change in the world, time, too, would be there, because change can only take place in time and is completely unthinkable without the presupposition of time.

Here now is represented an end of all things as objects of the senses whereof we can formulate absolutely no concept, because inevitably we entangle ourselves in contradictions if we choose to take one single step out of the sensible world into the intelligible. This happens through the fact that the moment which determines the end of the sensible world is also supposed to be the beginning of the intelligible world; therefore, the latter is brought into one and the same temporal series with the former, and this is self-contradictory.

334

But we also say that we conceive a duration as infinite (as eternity), not because we have any ascertainable concept at all of its enormity, for that is impossible since eternity lacks time altogether as a measure of itself; but rather, that concept is a purely negative one of the eternal duration, because where there is no time, also *no end* is possible. By means of this concept we do not proceed a single step further in our knowledge, but will have only declared that reason, in a practical sense, can never reach an ultimate purpose on the path of perpetual changes. And, too, if reason attempts it by employing the principle of rest and immutability of the condition of the world-creatures, it would not only be just as unsatisfactory with regard to its theoretical use but, rather, would end in total thoughtlessness. In these circumstances then nothing else remains for reason except to visualize a variation that progresses into the infinite (in time) within the perpetual progression toward the ultimate purpose in connection with which its *disposition* endures and is itself constant, a disposition which is

11 [In the King James Version verse three reads: "When he (the angel) had cried, seven thunders uttered their voices." A note tells us that the seven thunders is the voice of God speaking in judgment (cf. Rev. 12:27–31), not, as Kant says here, the voice of the angel.]

not mutable like that progression of a phenomenon, but is rather something supersensible and is, consequently, not fluctuating in time. The rule for the practical use of reason according to this Idea, therefore, intends to express nothing more than that we must take our maxims as if, in all its changes from good to better which proceed into the infinite, our moral state, with respect to its disposition (the *homo noumenon*, "whose change takes place in heaven") would not be subjected at all to temporal change.

But that some time a moment will make its appearance when all change—and with it time itself—will cease is a notion that revolts our imagination. Then, of course, the whole of nature, as it were, will grow rigid and petrified; then the final thought, the last feeling will remain stationary in the thinking subject and ever the same without variation. For a creature which can be conscious of its existence and the magnitude of it (viewed as a duration) in time only, such a life, if, indeed, it may be called life, must seem equivalent to annihilation, because in order to fancy itself in such a situation, the creature must really still contemplate something; but contemplation comprehends a process of reflection which itself can only occur in time. Hence the inhabitants of the other world, according to their dwelling place (heaven or hell), are presented as singing forever and ever the same song, either their hallelujah, or eternally doleful notes ([Rev.] 19:1-6; 20:15); in this way the total absence of all change is meant to be indicated in their state.

However much this Idea transcends our cognitive capacity, it is still closely akin to reason in a practical respect. If we accept the moral-physical condition of man here in life even on the best terms, that is to say, of a perpetual progression and advance to the highest good which is marked out as his destination, he still cannot (even in the consciousness of the immutability of his disposition) unite contentment with the prospect of his condition (moral as well as physical) enduring in an eternal state of change. For the condition in which man now exists remains ever an evil, in comparison to the better con-

dition into which he stands ready to proceed; and the notion
of an infinite progression to the ultimate purpose is still simultaneously one prospect in an unending series of evils which, if
they are truly outweighed by the greater good, yet do not permit contentment to prevail—a contentment which he can think
only by thinking that the ultimate purpose will some time
finally be reached.

Now as a result the speculative man becomes entangled in
mysticism where his reason does not understand itself and what
it wants, and rather prefers to dote on the beyond than to con-
fine itself within the bounds of this world, as is fitting for an
intellectual inhabitant of a sensible world; for reason, because
it is not easily satisfied with its immanent, that is, its practical,
use but likes to attempt something in the transcendent, also
has its mysteries. Thence arises Lao-kiun's monstrosity [12] of the
highest good which is supposed to consist in nihility [*im
Nichts*], that is, in the consciousness of feeling oneself swallowed up in the abyss of the Godhead through the fusion with
it, and, therefore, through the destruction of one's personality.
To have the presentiment of this condition, Chinese philosophers strive in dark rooms with eyes closed to experience and
contemplate their nihility. Thence the pantheism (of the
Tibetans and other Oriental peoples) and the subsequent
Spinozism engendered from the sublimation of pantheism,
both of which are closely akin to the primeval system of the
emanation of all human souls from the Godhead (and of their
final reabsorption into it). All of this merely so that people
might still ultimately have an eternal repose to delight in,
which then constitutes their presumed blissful end of all
things. At the same time this is really a concept in company   336
with which their understanding disintegrates and all thinking
itself comes to an end.

The end of all things which pass through men's hands even
if their purposes are good is folly, i.e., the use of means which
are opposed to the purposes they are supposed to serve. Wis-

[12] [Probably refers to Lao-Tsu (604?-531 B.C.), founder of the pantheistic
Taoist religion.]

dom, that is, practical wisdom, in the commensurateness of its measures which are in full accord with the ultimate purpose of all things, with the highest good, abides alone with God. And to respond to this Idea, by not obviously acting against it, is what we might perhaps call human wisdom. But this security against folly which the human being may hope to attain only through trials and frequent change of his plans is besides "a jewel which even the best man can only pursue *if he perchance desires to lay hold of it*"; but he never permits egotistic persuasion to come upon him, much less does he permit himself to act toward it as if he had laid hold of it. Thence [arise] the schemes—changing from time to time and often absurd—for appropriate means to make religion at once both pure and powerful in an entire nation, so that men can loudly proclaim: Miserable mortals, nothing is constant in your lives except inconstancy! [13]

Nevertheless, if, for once, these trials have finally succeeded so greatly that the commonwealth is willing and able to give ear, not merely to conventional doctrines of devotion, but also to practical reason which is illuminated by them (even as it is absolutely necessary to religion); if (in a human way) the sages among the people, rather than coming to an agreement among themselves (like a clergy), as fellow citizens draw up plans and agree upon them for the most part, this demonstrates in a trustworthy way that truth is of concern to them. And the nation, too, takes an interest in it on the whole (although not yet in the subtlest detail) owing to the generally sensed necessity—not based on authority—for the indispensable cultivation of its moral character [*Anlage*]. Thus nothing seems to be more advisable than to leave the sages alone to make and pursue their course since, for once, they are making satisfactory progress with respect to the *idea* to which they are attending; and to leave to Providence the outcome of the means selected to-

[13] [Kant alludes to a translation of a work by the French Jesuit, Gabriel F. Coyer (1707-82), which appeared in Berlin, 1761, under the title *Moralische Kleinigkeiten*. This thought appealed to him; he uses the same aphorism below, p. 141.]

ward the best ultimate purpose, since it remains always uncertain what the issue may be according to the course of nature. For we may be as incredulous as we wish, yet where it is absolutely impossible to see in advance with certainty the success that results from positive means which are accepted according to all human wisdom (which, if it deserves its name, must move solely toward morality), we must still give credence to a concurrence of divine wisdom with the course of nature in a practical sense, if we do not prefer to relinquish our ultimate purpose altogether. To be sure, people will object. Often it has been said that the present plan is the best; it is the one according to which things must endure for now and ever more; now it is a condition for eternity. "Whoever (according to this concept) is good, is always good, and whoever (contrary to it) is evil, is always evil" (Rev. 22:11): [14] exactly as if eternity, and with it, the end of all things could already be entered now. And yet, since that time, continually new schemes have been introduced, among which the newest was often only the revival of an old one; and henceforward also there will be no lack of more final projects.

I am so very conscious of my inability to make a new and successful attempt in this, lacking as I do any great inventive faculty for it, that I prefer to counsel people to leave matters just as they last stood and as they had, throughout almost a generation, proved bearable in their consequences. But since that probably may not be the opinion of men of either an eminent or at least an enterprising spirit, allow me to note discreetly not so much what they would have to do, but rather against what they would have to beware of offending, because otherwise they would be acting contrary to their own aim (even if it were the best).

Christianity has something worthy of love [*Liebenswürdiges*] about it, beside the deepest respect which the sanctity of its

14 [The full verse in the King James Version reads: "He that is unjust, let him be unjust still: and he which is filthy, let him be filthy still: and he that is righteous, let him be righteous still: and he that is holy, let him be holy still."]

laws irresistibly inspires. (I do not mean here the worthiness of love [*Liebenswürdigkeit*] of the person, which Christianity through great sacrifices procured for us, but rather that of the thing itself, namely, the moral organization that He instituted; for the former may only be inferred from the latter.) [15] Respect is undoubtedly the primary thing, because without it there also cannot be any genuine love, although one person can still cherish great respect toward another without love. However, if it is a question not simply of the notion of duty, but also of adherence to duty—if we ask after the subjective motive for actions from which, if we may assume it, the first thing to anticipate is what the man will do, and not merely ask after the objective motive, which would tell us *what he should do*— then love as the free reception of the will of another person into one's own maxims will certainly be an indispensable complement to the imperfection of human nature (the imperfection being that human nature must be constrained to do that which reason prescribes through law). For what a person does unwillingly he does so poorly, even resorting to sophistic subterfuges to evade the precept of duty, that this latter may not be relied on very much as a motive without the participation of love.

If now, in order to perfect it, we add some further authority to Christianity (be it divine even), let the intention behind it be ever so well-meaning and its purpose ever so genuinely good, still its worthiness of love has vanished; for it is a contradiction to command someone not just to do something but also to do it willingly.

Christianity aims to promote love for the observance of its duty in general and elicits it, too, because the founder of this religion speaks not in the character of a dictator who impresses people by a will that demands obedience, but speaks rather in the character of a humanitarian [*Menschenfreundes*] who brings to the heart of his fellowmen their own well-understood

---

[15] [The sentence is obscure; we have translated literally.]

[*wohlverstandenen*] wills, according to which they would act spontaneously of themselves if they proved themselves fitting.

It is, therefore, the *liberal* way of thinking—equidistant from both the sense of servitude and anarchy—whereof Christianity anticipates an effect for its teachings. With this approach it is able to win to itself the hearts of men whose understanding is already illuminated by the conception of the law of their duty. The feeling of freedom in the choice of their ultimate purpose is what makes the legislation worthy of their love. Therefore, although the teacher of Christianity likewise proclaims punishments, we are not to understand that they were meant to become the motives to cause us to comply with its commandments; at all events, an explanation of this sort certainly is not in keeping with the peculiar quality of Christianity. For insofar as this were so, Christianity would cease to be worthy of love. We may explain this rather only as a generous warning arising out of the legislator's good will, to be on our guard against the damage which should inevitably spring from the transgression of the law (for *lex est res surda et inexorabilis,* Livy [16]). Since Christianity, viewed as an assemblage of voluntarily received maxims of life, does not threaten here, while the law does, the law as the immutable order which lies in the nature of things has not left to the choice even of the Creator the determination of the consequences of it this way or that.

339

If Christianity promises rewards (for example, "Rejoice and be exceeding glad: for great is your reward in Heaven" [17]), this must not be explained, according to the liberal way of thinking, as if it were an offer to bribe the man, as it were, to exhibit good conduct; for then again Christianity would not be intrinsically worthy of love. Only a desire for such actions which

---

[16] [The passage to which Kant is referring reads *leges rem surdam, inexorabilem esse, salubriorem, melioremque inopi quam potenti:* "The law was a thing without ears, inexorable, more salutary and serviceable to the pauper than to the great man" (Livy II. 3. 4, trans. B. O. Foster, "Loeb Classical Library" edn.).]

[17] [Matt. 5:12.]

arise from disinterested motives can inspire human respect toward the one who does this desiring; and without respect there
is no true love. Therefore, we must not think that the promised
rewards are intended to be taken for the incentives of the actions. The love, whereby a liberal way of thinking is bound to
a benefactor, is guided not by the good which the needy person receives, but simply by the goodness of the benefactor's will
which is inclined to confer it, even if perchance he should not
have the power for it or is hindered in its realization by other
motives devoted to the general good of the world.

That is the moral worthiness of love which Christianity
carries within itself, which still glimmers through the many
constraints appended to it with the very frequent change of
opinions. It has preserved Christianity itself in the face of the
aversion which it otherwise would have encountered, and (what
is remarkable) this worthiness shows itself in a light only so
much the brighter at the time of the greatest enlightenment
which ever was among men.

Should Christianity once reach the point where it ceases to
be worthy of love (which might well happen if it were armed
with dictatorial authority instead of its gentle spirit), then a
natural antipathy and insubordination toward it would be
bound to become the predominant mode of men's thinking,
since no neutrality prevails in matters of morality (still less a
coalition of conflicting principles). And the Antichrist, who
is considered to be the harbinger of Doomsday, would take up
his reign (presumably founded on fear and selfishness). Then,
however, Christianity, though indeed intended to be the universal world religion, would not be favored by the workings of
fate to become so, and the (perverse) end of all things (in a
moral point of view) would come to pass.[18]

[18] [This follows emendations to the last two sentences given in the
Akademie edn., VIII, 505.]

Whether this satirical inscription on a Dutch innkeeper's sign upon which a burial ground was painted had for its object mankind in general, or the rulers of states in particular, who are insatiable of war, or merely the philosophers who dream this sweet dream, it is not for us to decide. But one condition the author of this essay wishes to lay down. The practical politician assumes the attitude of looking down with great self-satisfaction on the political theorist as a pedant whose empty ideas in no way threaten the security of the state, inasmuch as the state must proceed on empirical principles; so the theorist is allowed to play his game without interference from the worldly-wise statesman. Such being his attitude, the practical politician —and this is the condition I make—should at least act consistently in the case of a conflict and not suspect some danger to the state in the political theorist's opinions which are ventured and publicly expressed without any ulterior purpose. By this *clausula salvatoria* the author desires formally and emphatically to deprecate herewith any malevolent interpretation which might be placed on his words.

SECTION I

CONTAINING THE PRELIMINARY ARTICLES FOR PERPETUAL PEACE AMONG STATES

1. *"No Treaty of Peace Shall Be Held Valid in Which There Is Tacitly Reserved Matter for a Future War"*

Otherwise a treaty would be only a truce, a suspension of hostilities but not peace, which means the end of all hostilities—so much so that even to attach the word "perpetual" to it is a dubious pleonasm. The causes for making future wars (which are perhaps unknown to the contracting parties) are without exception annihilated by the treaty of peace, even if they should be dug out of dusty documents by acute sleuthing. When one or both parties to a treaty of peace, being too exhausted to continue warring with each other, make a tacit reservation (*reservatio mentalis*) in regard to old claims to be elaborated only at some more favorable opportunity in the future, the treaty is made in bad faith, and we have an artifice worthy of the casuistry of a Jesuit. Considered by itself, it is beneath the dignity of a sovereign, just as the readiness to indulge in this kind of reasoning is unworthy of the dignity of his minister.

But if, in consequence of enlightened concepts of statecraft, the glory of the state is placed in its continual aggrandizement by whatever means, my conclusion will appear merely academic and pedantic.

2. *"No Independent States, Large or Small, Shall Come under the Dominion of Another State by Inheritance, Exchange, Purchase, or Donation"*

A state is not, like the ground which it occupies, a piece of property (*patrimonium*). It is a society of men whom no one else has any right to command or to dispose except the state itself. It is a trunk with its own roots. But to incorporate it into another state, like a graft, is to destroy its existence as a moral person, reducing it to a thing; such incorporation thus contradicts the idea of the original contract without which no right over a people can be conceived.[1]

---

[1] A hereditary kingdom is not a state which can be inherited by another state, but the right to govern it can be inherited by another physical person. The state thereby acquires a ruler, but he, as a ruler (i.e., as one already possessing another realm), does not acquire the state.

Everyone knows to what dangers Europe, the only part of the world where this manner of acquisition is known, has been brought, even down to the most recent times, by the presumption that states could espouse one another; it is in part a new kind of industry for gaining ascendancy by means of family alliances and without expenditure of forces, and in part a way of extending one's domain. Also the hiring-out of troops by one state to another, so that they can be used against an enemy not common to both, is to be counted under this principle; [2] for in this manner the subjects, as though they were things to be manipulated at pleasure, are used and also used up.

3. "Standing Armies (miles perpetuus) Shall in Time Be Totally Abolished"

345

For they incessantly menace other states by their readiness to appear at all times prepared for war; they incite them to compete with each other in the number of armed men, and there is no limit to this. For this reason, the cost of peace finally becomes more oppressive than that of a short war, and consequently a standing army is itself a cause of offensive war waged in order to relieve the state of this burden. Add to this that to pay men to kill or to be killed seems to entail using them as mere machines and tools in the hand of another (the state), and this is hardly compatible with the rights of mankind in our own person. But the periodic and voluntary military exercises of citizens who thereby secure themselves and their country against foreign aggression are entirely different.

The accumulation of treasure would have the same effect, for, of the three powers—the power of armies, of alliances, and of money—the third is perhaps the most depend-

2 [This is an obvious reference to the hiring-out of the Hessians to England in the American Revolutionary War only a few years before this treatise was written.]

able weapon.[3] Such accumulation of treasure is regarded by other states as a threat of war, and if it were not for the difficulties in learning the amount, it would force the other state to make an early attack.

4. *"National Debts Shall Not Be Contracted with a View to the External Friction of States"*

This expedient of seeking aid within or without the state is above suspicion when the purpose is domestic economy (e.g., the improvement of roads, new settlements, establishment of stores against unfruitful years, etc.). But as an opposing machine in the antagonism of powers, a credit system which grows beyond sight and which is yet a safe debt for the present requirements—because all the creditors do not require payment at one time—constitutes a dangerous money power. This ingenious invention of a commercial people [England] in this century is dangerous because it is a war treasure which exceeds the treasures of all other states; it cannot be exhausted except by default of taxes (which is inevitable), though it can be long delayed by the stimulus to trade which occurs through the reaction of credit on industry and commerce. This facility in making war, together with the inclination to do so on the part of rulers—an inclination which seems inborn in human nature—is thus a great hindrance to perpetual peace. Therefore, to forbid this credit system must be a preliminary article of perpetual peace all the more because it must eventually entangle many innocent states in the inevitable bankruptcy and openly harm them. They are therefore justified in allying themselves against such a state and its measures.

346

[3] [This is probably a reference to the mercantilistic policy of Frederick William I, who collected a state treasure which in turn gave Frederick the Great the means to wage the Seven Years War.]

5. *"No State Shall by Force Interfere with the Constitution or Government of Another State"*

For what is there to authorize it to do so? The offense, perhaps, which a state gives to the subjects of another state? Rather the example of the evil into which a state has fallen because of its lawlessness should serve as a warning. Moreover, the bad example which one free person affords another as a *scandalum acceptum* is not an infringement of his rights. But it would be quite different if a state, by internal rebellion, should fall into two parts, each of which pretended to be a separate state making claim to the whole. To lend assistance to one of these cannot be considered an interference in the constitution of the other state (for it is then in a state of anarchy). But so long as the internal dissension has not come to this critical point, such interference by foreign powers would infringe on the rights of an independent people struggling with its internal disease; hence it would itself be an offense and would render the autonomy of all states insecure.

6. *"No State Shall, during War, Permit Such Acts of Hostility Which Would Make Mutual Confidence in the Subsequent Peace Impossible: Such Are the Employment of Assassins* (percussores), *Poisoners* (venefici), *Breach of Capitulation, and Incitement to Treason* (perduellio) *in the Opposing State"*

These are dishonorable stratagems. For some confidence in the character of the enemy must remain even in the midst of war, as otherwise no peace could be concluded and the hostilities would degenerate into a war of extermination (*bellum internecinum*). War, however, is only the sad recourse in the state of nature (where there is no tribunal which could judge with the force of law) by which each state asserts its right by violence and in which neither party can be adjudged unjust (for that would presuppose a

347

juridical decision); in lieu of such a decision, the issue of the conflict (as if given by a so-called "judgment of God") decides on which side justice lies. But between states no punitive war (*bellum punitivum*) is conceivable, because there is no relation between them of master and servant.

It follows that a war of extermination, in which the destruction of both parties and of all justice can result, would permit perpetual peace only in the vast burial ground of the human race. Therefore, such a war and the use of all means leading to it must be absolutely forbidden. But that the means cited do inevitably lead to it is clear from the fact that these infernal arts, vile in themselves, when once used would not long be confined to the sphere of war. Take, for instance, the use of spies (*uti exploratoribus*). In this, one employs the infamy of others (which can never be entirely eradicated) only to encourage its persistence even into the state of peace, to the undoing of the very spirit of peace.

Although the laws stated are objectively, i.e., in so far as they express the intention of rulers, mere prohibitions (*leges prohibitivae*), some of them are of that strict kind which hold regardless of circumstances (*leges strictae*) and which demand prompt execution. Such are Nos. 1, 5, and 6. Others, like Nos. 2, 3, and 4, while not exceptions from the rule of law, nevertheless are subjectively broader (*leges latae*) in respect to their observation, containing permission to delay their execution without, however, losing sight of the end. This permission does not authorize, under No. 2, for example, delaying until doomsday (or, as Augustus used to say, *ad calendas Graecas*) the re-establishment of the freedom of states which have been deprived of it—i.e., it does not permit us to fail to do it, but it allows a delay to prevent precipitation which might injure the goal striven for. For the prohibition concerns only the manner of acquisition which is no longer permitted, but not the possession, which, though not bearing a requisite title of right, has nevertheless been held lawful in all states by the public opinion of the time (the time of the putative acquisition).[4]

348

[4] It has not without cause hitherto been doubted whether besides the commands (*leges praeceptivae*) and prohibitions (*leges prohibitivae*) there could also be permissive laws (*leges permissivae*) of pure reason. For laws as such contain a principle of objective practical necessity, while permission implies a principle of the practical contingency of certain actions. Hence a law of permission would imply constraint to an action to do that to which no one can be constrained. If the object of the law has the same meaning in both cases, this is a contradiction. But in permissive law, which is in question here, the prohibition refers only to the future mode of acquisition of a right (e.g., by succession), while the permission annuls this prohibition only with reference to the present possession. This possession, though only putative, may be held to be just (*possessio putativa*) in the transition from the state of nature to a civil state, by virtue of a permissive law included under natural law, even though it is [strictly] illegal. But, as soon as it is recognized as illegal in the state of nature, a similar mode of acquisition in the subsequent civil state (after this transition has occurred) is forbidden, and this right to continuing possession would not hold if such a presumptive acquisition had taken place in the civil state. For in this case it would be an infringement which would have to cease as soon as its illegality was discovered.

I have wished only to call the attention of the teachers of natural law to the concept of a *lex permissiva*, which systematic reason affords, particularly since in civil (statute) law use is often made of it. But in the ordinary use of it, there is this difference: prohibitive law stands alone, while permission is not introduced into it as a limiting condition (as it should be) but counted among the exceptions to it. Then it is said, "This or that is forbidden, except Nos. 1, 2, 3," and so on indefinitely. These exceptions are added to the law only as an afterthought required by our groping around among cases as they arise, and not by any principle. Otherwise the conditions would have had to be introduced into the formula of the prohibition, and in this way it would itself have become a permissive law. It is, therefore, unfortunate that the subtle question proposed by the wise and acute Count von Windischgrätz * was never answered and soon consigned to oblivion, because it insisted on the point here discussed. For the possibility

* [Reichsgraf Josef Niklas von Windischgrätz (1744-1802) proposed the following question for a prize essay: "How can contracts be drawn which will be susceptible to no divergent interpretation, and by which any suit concerning transfer of property will be impossible, so that no legal process can arise from any document having this proposed form?"]

SECTION II

CONTAINING THE DEFINITIVE ARTICLES FOR PERPETUAL PEACE AMONG STATES

348   The state of peace among men living side by side is not
the natural state (*status naturalis*); the natural state is one
349 of war. This does not always mean open hostilities, but at
least an unceasing threat of war. A state of peace, therefore, must be *established,* for in order to be secured against
hostility it is not sufficient that hostilities simply be not
committed; and, unless this security is pledged to each by
his neighbor (a thing that can occur only in a civil state),
each may treat his neighbor, from whom he demands this
security, as an enemy.[1]

---

of a formula similar to those of mathematics is the only legitimate
criterion of a consistent legislation, and without it the so-called *ius
certum* must always remain a pious wish. Otherwise we shall have
merely general laws (which apply to a great number of cases), but no
universal laws (which apply to all cases) as the concept of a law seems
to require.

[1] We ordinarily assume that no one may act inimically toward another except when he has been actively injured by the other. This is
quite correct if both are under civil law, for, by entering into such a
state, they afford each other the requisite security through the sovereign
which has power over both. Man (or the people) in the state of nature
deprives me of this security and injures me, if he is near me, by this
mere status of his, even though he does not injure me actively (*facto*);
he does so by the lawlessness of his condition (*statu iniusto*) which
constantly threatens me. Therefore, I can compel him either to enter
with me into a state of civil law or to remove himself from my neighborhood. The postulate which is basic to all the following articles is:
All men who can reciprocally influence each other must stand under
some civil constitution.

Every juridical constitution which concerns the person who stands
under it is one of the following:

(1) The constitution conforming to the civil law of men in a nation (*ius civitatis*).

FIRST DEFINITIVE ARTICLE FOR PERPETUAL PEACE

"The Civil Constitution of Every State Should Be Republican"

The only constitution which derives from the idea of the original compact, and on which all juridical legislation of a people must be based, is the republican.[2] This constitu- 350

---

(2) The constitution conforming to the law of nations in their relation to one another (*ius gentium*).

(3) The constitution conforming to the law of world citizenship, so far as men and states are considered as citizens of a universal state of men, in their external mutual relationships (*ius cosmopoliticum*).

This division is not arbitrary, being necessary in relation to the idea of perpetual peace. For if only one state were related to another by physical influence and were yet in a state of nature, war would necessarily follow, and our purpose here is precisely to free ourselves of war.

2 Juridical (and hence) external freedom cannot be defined, as is 350 usual, by the privilege of doing anything one wills so long as he does not injure another. For what is a privilege? It is the possibility of an action so far as one does not injure anyone by it. Then the definition would read: Freedom is the possibility of those actions by which one does no one an injury. One does another no injury (he may do as he pleases) only if he does another no injury—an empty tautology. Rather, my external (juridical) freedom is to be defined as follows: It is the privilege to lend obedience to no external laws except those to which I could have given consent. Similarly, external (juridical) equality in a state is that relationship among the citizens in which no one can lawfully bind another without at the same time subjecting himself to the law by which he also can be bound. No definition of juridical dependence is needed, as this already lies in the concept of a state's constitution as such.

The validity of these inborn rights, which are inalienable and belong necessarily to humanity, is raised to an even higher level by the principle of the juridical relation of man to higher beings, for, if he believes in them, he regards himself by the same principles as a citizen of a supersensuous world. For in what concerns my freedom, I have no obligation with respect to divine law, which can be acknowledged by my reason alone, except in so far as I could have given my consent to it. Indeed, it is only through the law of freedom of my own reason that I frame a concept of the divine will. With regard to

tion is established, firstly, by principles of the freedom of
the members of a society (as men); secondly, by principles
of dependence of all upon a single common legislation (as
subjects); and, thirdly, by the law of their equality (as citizens). The republican constitution, therefore, is, with respect to law, the one which is the original basis of every
form of civil constitution. The only question now is: Is it
also the one which can lead to perpetual peace?

351   The republican constitution, besides the purity of its
origin (having sprung from the pure source of the concept
of law), also gives a favorable prospect for the desired consequence, i.e., perpetual peace. The reason is this: if the
consent of the citizens is required in order to decide that
war should be declared (and in this constitution it cannot
but be the case), nothing is more natural than that they
would be very cautious in commencing such a poor game,

---

the most sublime reason in the world that I can think of, with the
exception of God—say, the great Aeon—when I do my duty in my post
as he does in his, there is no reason under the law of equality why
obedience to duty should fall only to me and the right to command
only to him. The reason why this principle of equality does not pertain to our relation to God (as the principle of freedom does) is that
this Being is the only one to which the concept of duty does not
apply.

    But with respect to the right of equality of all citizens as subjects,
the question of whether a hereditary nobility may be tolerated turns
351 upon the answer to the question as to whether the pre-eminent rank
granted by the state to one citizen over another ought to precede
merit or follow it. Now it is obvious that, if rank is associated with
birth, it is uncertain whether merit (political skill and integrity) will
also follow; hence it would be as if a favorite without any merit were
given command. The general will of the people would never agree to
this in the original contract, which is the principle of all law, for a
nobleman is not necessarily a noble man. With regard to the nobility
of office (as we might call the rank of the higher magistracy) which
one must earn by merit, this rank does not belong to the person as
his property; it belongs to his post, and equality is not thereby infringed, because when a man quits his office he renounces the rank it
confers and re-enters into the class of his fellows.

decreeing for themselves all the calamities of war. Among the latter would be: having to fight, having to pay the costs of war from their own resources, having painfully to repair the devastation war leaves behind, and, to fill up the measure of evils, load themselves with a heavy national debt that would embitter peace itself and that can never be liquidated on account of constant wars in the future. But, on the other hand, in a constitution which is not republican, and under which the subjects are not citizens, a declaration of war is the easiest thing in the world to decide upon, because war does not require of the ruler, who is the proprietor and not a member of the state, the least sacrifice of the pleasures of his table, the chase, his country houses, his court functions, and the like. He may, therefore, resolve on war as on a pleasure party for the most trivial reasons, and with perfect indifference leave the justification which decency requires to the diplomatic corps who are ever ready to provide it.

In order not to confuse the republican constitution with the democratic (as is commonly done), the following should be noted. The forms of a state (*civitas*) can be divided   352 either according to the persons who possess the sovereign power or according to the mode of administration exercised over the people by the chief, whoever he may be. The first is properly called the form of sovereignty (*forma imperii*), and there are only three possible forms of it: autocracy, in which one, aristocracy, in which some associated together, or democracy, in which all those who constitute society, possess sovereign power. They may be characterized, respectively, as the power of a monarch, of the nobility, or of the people. The second division is that by the form of government (*forma regiminis*) and is based on the way in which the state makes use of its power; this way is based on the constitution, which is the act of the general will through which the many persons become one nation.

In this respect government is either republican or despotic. Republicanism is the political principle of the separation of the executive power (the administration) from the legislative; despotism is that of the autonomous execution by the state of laws which it has itself decreed. Thus in a despotism the public will is administered by the ruler as his own will. Of the three forms of the state, that of democracy is, properly speaking, necessarily a despotism, because it establishes an executive power in which "all" decide for or even against one who does not agree; that is, "all," who are not quite all, decide, and this is a contradiction of the general will with itself and with freedom.

Every form of government which is not representative is, properly speaking, without form. The legislator can unite in one and the same person his function as legislative and as executor of his will just as little as the universal of the major premise in a syllogism can also be the subsumption of the particular under the universal in the minor. And even though the other two constitutions are always defective to the extent that they do leave room for this mode of administration, it is at least possible for them to assume a mode of government conforming to the spirit of a representative system (as when Frederick II [3] at least *said* he was merely the first servant of the state).[4] On the other hand, 353   the democratic mode of government makes this impossible, since everyone wishes to be master. Therefore, we can say:

[3] [Frederick the Great, in his *Anti-Macchiavel.*]

[4] The lofty epithets of "the Lord's anointed," "the executor of the divine will on earth," and "the vicar of God," which have been lavished on sovereigns, have been frequently censured as crude and intoxicating flatteries. But this seems to me without good reason. Far 353   from inspiring a monarch with pride, they should rather render him humble, providing he possesses some intelligence (which we must assume). They should make him reflect that he has taken an office too great for man, an office which is the holiest God has ordained on earth, to be the trustee of the rights of men, and that he must always stand in dread of having in some way injured this "apple of God's eye."

the smaller the personnel of the government (the smaller the number of rulers), the greater is their representation and the more nearly the constitution approaches to the possibility of republicanism; thus the constitution may be expected by gradual reform finally to raise itself to republicanism. For these reasons it is more difficult for an aristocracy than for a monarchy to achieve the one completely juridical constitution, and it is impossible for a democracy to do so except by violent revolution.

The mode of government,[5] however, is incomparably more important to the people than the form of sovereignty, although much depends on the greater or lesser suitability of the latter to the end of [good] government. To conform to the concept of law, however, government must have a representative form, and in this system only a republican mode of government is possible; without it, government is despotic and arbitrary, whatever the constitution may be. None of the ancient so-called "republics" knew this system, and they all finally and inevitably degenerated into despotism under the sovereignty of one, which is the most bearable of all forms of despotism.

[5] Mallet du Pan,[*] in his pompous but empty and hollow language, pretends to have become convinced, after long experience, of the truth of Pope's well-known saying:

"For forms of government let fools contest:
Whate'er is best administered, is best." [†]

If that means that the best-administered state is the state that is best administered, he has, to make use of Swift's expression, "cracked a nut to come at a maggot." But if it means that the best-administered state also has the best mode of government, i.e., the best constitution, then it is thoroughly wrong, for examples of good governments prove nothing about the form of government. Whoever reigned better than a Titus and a Marcus Aurelius? Yet one was succeeded by a Domitian and the other by a Commodus. This could never have happened under a good constitution, for their unworthiness for this post was known early enough and also the power of the ruler was sufficient to have excluded them.

[*] [Jacques Mallet du Pan (1749-1800), in his *Über die französische Revolution und die Ursachen ihrer Dauer* (1794).]

[†] [*Essay on Man,* III, 303-4.]

SECOND DEFINITIVE ARTICLE FOR A PERPETUAL PEACE

"The Law of Nations Shall be Founded on a Federation of Free States"

354   Peoples, as states, like individuals, may be judged to injure one another merely by their coexistence in the state of
nature (i.e., while independent of external laws). Each of
them may and should for the sake of its own security demand that the others enter with it into a constitution similar to the civil constitution, for under such a constitution
each can be secure in his right. This would be a league of
nations, but it would not have to be a state consisting of
nations. That would be contradictory, since a state implies
the relation of a superior (legislating) to an inferior (obeying), i.e., the people, and many nations in one state would
then constitute only one nation. This contradicts the presupposition, for here we have to weigh the rights of nations against each other so far as they are distinct states
and not amalgamated into one.

When we see the attachment of savages to their lawless
freedom, preferring ceaseless combat to subjection to a lawful constraint which they might establish, and thus preferring senseless freedom to rational freedom, we regard it
with deep contempt as barbarity, rudeness, and a brutish
degradation of humanity. Accordingly, one would think
that civilized people (each united in a state) would hasten
all the more to escape, the sooner the better, from such a
depraved condition. But, instead, each state places its majesty (for it is absurd to speak of the majesty of the people)
in being subject to no external juridical restraint, and the
splendor of its sovereign consists in the fact that many
thousands stand at his command to sacrifice themselves for
something that does not concern them and without his
needing to place himself in the least danger.[6] The chief

6 A Bulgarian prince gave the following answer to the Greek emperor who good-naturedly suggested that they settle their difference

difference between European and American savages lies in the fact that many tribes of the latter have been eaten by their enemies, while the former know how to make better use of their conquered enemies than to dine off them; they know better how to use them to increase the number of 355 their subjects and thus the quantity of instruments for even more extensive wars.

When we consider the perverseness of human nature which is nakedly revealed in the uncontrolled relations between nations (this perverseness being veiled in the state of civil law by the constraint exercised by government), we may well be astonished that the word "law" has not yet been banished from war politics as pedantic, and that no state has yet been bold enough to advocate this point of view. Up to the present, Hugo Grotius, Pufendorf, Vattel,[7] and many other irritating comforters have been cited in justification of war, though their code, philosophically or diplomatically formulated, has not and cannot have the least legal force, because states as such do not stand under a common external power. There is no instance on record that a state has ever been moved to desist from its purpose because of arguments backed up by the testimony of such great men. But the homage which each state pays (at least in words) to the concept of law proves that there is slumbering in man an even greater moral disposition to become master of the evil principle in himself (which he cannot disclaim) and to hope for the same from others. Otherwise the word "law" would never be pronounced by states which wish to war upon one another; it would be used only ironically, as a Gallic prince interpreted it when he said, "It is

---

by a duel: "A smith who has tongs won't pluck the glowing iron from the fire with his bare hands."

[7] [Hugo Grotius (1583-1645), Samuel von Pufendorf (1632-1694), and Emer de Vattel (1714-1767) developed systems of international law which recognized the legitimacy of some wars. See Grotius, *De jure belli ac pacis* (1625), Pufendorf, *De jure naturae et gentium* (1672), Vattel, *Le Droit des gens* (1758).]

the prerogative which nature has given the stronger that the weaker should obey him."

States do not plead their cause before a tribunal; war alone is their way of bringing suit. But by war and its favorable issue in victory, right is not decided, and though by a treaty of peace this particular war is brought to an end, the state of war, of always finding a new pretext to hostilities, is not terminated. Nor can this be declared wrong, considering the fact that in this state each is the judge of his own case. Notwithstanding, the obligation which men in a lawless condition have under the natural law, and which requires them to abandon the state of nature, does not quite apply to states under the law of nations, for as states they already have an internal juridical constitution and have thus outgrown compulsion from others to submit to a more extended lawful constitution according to their ideas of right. This is true in spite of the fact that reason, from its throne of supreme moral legislating authority, absolutely condemns war as a legal recourse and makes a state of peace a direct duty, even though peace cannot be established or secured except by a compact among nations.

356

For these reasons there must be a league of a particular kind, which can be called a league of peace (*foedus pacificum*), and which would be distinguished from a treaty of peace (*pactum pacis*) by the fact that the latter terminates only one war, while the former seeks to make an end of all wars forever. This league does not tend to any dominion over the power of the state but only to the maintenance and security of the freedom of the state itself and of other states in league with it, without there being any need for them to submit to civil laws and their compulsion, as men in a state of nature must submit.

The practicability (objective reality) of this idea of federation, which should gradually spread to all states and thus lead to perpetual peace, can be proved. For if fortune directs that a powerful and enlightened people can make itself a republic, which by its nature must be inclined to perpetual peace, this gives a fulcrum to the federation with other states so that they may adhere to it and thus secure freedom under the idea of the law of nations. By more and more such associations, the federation may be gradually extended.

We may readily conceive that a people should say, "There ought to be no war among us, for we want to make ourselves into a state; that is, we want to establish a supreme legislative, executive, and judiciary power which will reconcile our differences peaceably." But when this state says, "There ought to be no war between myself and other states, even though I acknowledge no supreme legislative power by which our rights are mutually guaranteed," it is not at all clear on what I can base my confidence in my own rights unless it is the free federation, the surrogate of the civil social order, which reason necessarily associates with the concept of the law of nations—assuming that something is really meant by the latter.

The concept of a law of nations as a right to make war does not really mean anything, because it is then a law of deciding what is right by unilateral maxims through force 357 and not by universally valid public laws which restrict the freedom of each one. The only conceivable meaning of such a law of nations might be that it serves men right who are so inclined that they should destroy each other and thus find perpetual peace in the vast grave that swallows both the atrocities and their perpetrators. For states in their relation to each other, there cannot be any reasonable way out of the lawless condition which entails only war except that they, like individual men, should give up their savage (lawless) freedom, adjust themselves to the constraints of public law, and thus establish a continuously growing state consisting of various nations (civitas gentium), which will ultimately include all the nations of the world. But under the idea of the law of nations they do not wish this, and reject in practice what is correct in theory. If all is not to be lost, there can be, then, in place of the positive idea of a world republic, only the negative surrogate of an alliance which averts war, endures, spreads, and holds back the stream of those hostile passions which fear the law, though such an alliance is in constant peril of their breaking loose again.[8] *Furor impius intus . . . fremit horridus ore cruento* (Virgil).[9]

THIRD DEFINITIVE ARTICLE FOR A PERPETUAL PEACE

"The Law of World Citizenship Shall Be Limited to Conditions of Universal Hospitality"

358 Here, as in the preceding articles, it is not a question of philanthropy but of right. Hospitality means the right of a stranger not to be treated as an enemy when he arrives in the land of another. One may refuse to receive him when this can be done without causing his destruction; but, so long as he peacefully occupies his place, one may not treat him with hostility. It is not the right to be a permanent

---

[8] It would not ill become a people that has just terminated a war to decree, besides a day of thanksgiving, a day of fasting in order to ask heaven, in the name of the state, for forgiveness for the great iniquity which the human race still goes on to perpetuate in refusing to submit to a lawful constitution in their relation to other peoples, preferring, from pride in their independence, to make use of the barbarous means of war even though they are not able to attain what is sought, namely, the rights of a single state. The thanksgiving for victory won during the war, the hymns which are sung to the God of Hosts (in good Israelitic manner), stand in equally sharp contrast to the moral idea of the Father of Men. For they not only show a sad enough indifference to the way in which nations seek their rights, but in addition express a joy in having annihilated a multitude of men or their happiness.

[9] ["Within, impious Rage, sitting on savage arms, his hands fast bound behind with a hundred brazen knots, shall roar in the ghastliness of blood-stained lips" (*Aeneid* I, 294-96, trans. H. Rushton Fairclough, "Loeb Classical Library" edn.).]

visitor that one may demand. A special beneficent agreement would be needed in order to give an outsider a right
to become a fellow inhabitant for a certain length of time.
It is only a right of temporary sojourn, a right to associate,
which all men have. They have it by virtue of their common possession of the surface of the earth, where, as a
globe, they cannot infinitely disperse and hence must finally tolerate the presence of each other. Originally, no
one had more right than another to a particular part of
the earth.

Uninhabitable parts of the earth—the sea and the deserts
—divide this community of all men, but the ship and the
camel (the desert ship) enable them to approach each other
across these unruled regions and to establish communication by using the common right to the face of the earth,
which belongs to human beings generally. The inhospitality of the inhabitants of coasts (for instance, of the Barbary
Coast) in robbing ships in neighboring seas or enslaving
stranded travelers, or the inhospitality of the inhabitants
of the deserts (for instance, the Bedouin Arabs) who view
contact with nomadic tribes as conferring the right to plun-
der them, is thus opposed to natural law, even though it
extends the right of hospitality, i.e., the privilege of foreign
arrivals, no further than to conditions of the possibility of
seeking to communicate with the prior inhabitants. In this
way distant parts of the world can come into peaceable relations with each other, and these are finally publicly established by law. Thus the human race can gradually be
brought closer and closer to a constitution establishing
world citizenship.

But to this perfection compare the inhospitable actions
of the civilized and especially of the commercial states of
our part of the world. The injustice which they show to
lands and peoples they visit (which is equivalent to conquering them) is carried by them to terrifying lengths.
America, the lands inhabited by the Negro, the Spice
Islands, the Cape, etc., were at the time of their discovery

considered by these civilized intruders as lands without owners, for they counted the inhabitants as nothing. In East India (Hindustan), under the pretense of establishing economic undertakings, they brought in foreign soldiers

359 and used them to oppress the natives, excited widespread wars among the various states, spread famine, rebellion, perfidy, and the whole litany of evils which afflict mankind.

China [10] and Japan (Nippon), who have had experience

[10] To call this great empire by the name it gives itself, namely "China" and not "Sina" or anything like that, we have only to refer to [A.] Georgi, *Alphabetum Tibetanum*, pp. 651-54, especially note b. According to the note of Professor [Johann Eberhard] Fischer of Petersburg, there is no definite word used in that country as its name; the most usual word is "Kin," i.e., gold (which the Tibetans call "Ser"). Accordingly, the emperor is called "the king of gold," that is, king of the most splendid country in the world. In the empire itself, this word may be pronounced *Chin*, while because of the guttural sound the Italian missionaries may have called it *Kin.*—It is clear that what the Romans called the "Land of Seres" was China; the silk, however, was sent to Europe across Greater Tibet (through Lesser Tibet, Bukhara, Persia, and then on).

This suggests many reflections concerning the antiquity of this wonderful state, in comparison with that of Hindustan at the time of its union with Tibet and thence with Japan. We see, on the contrary, that the name "Sina" or "Tshina," said to have been used by the neighbors of the country, suggests nothing.

Perhaps we can also explain the very ancient but never well-known intercourse of Europe with Tibet by considering the shout, Κονξ 'Ομπαξ ("*Konx Ompax*"), of the hierophants in the Eleusinian mys-

360 teries, as we learn from Hysichius (cf. *Travels of the Young Anachar-sis*, Part V, p. 447 ff.). For, according to Georgi, *op. cit.*, the word *Concoia* means God, which has a striking resemblance to *Konx*. *Pah-cio* (*ibid.*, 520), which the Greeks may well have pronounced *pax*, means the *promulgator legis*, divinity pervading the whole of nature (also called *Cencresi*, p. 177). *Om*, however, which La Croze translates as *benedictus* ("blessed"), when applied to divinity perhaps means "the beatified" (p. 507). P. Franz Orazio often asked the Lamas of Tibet what they understood by "God" (*Concoia*) and always got the answer, "It is the assembly of saints" (i.e., the assembly of the blessed ones who, according to the doctrine of rebirth, finally, after many wander-ings through bodies of all kinds, have returned to God, or *Burchane*; that is to say, they are transmigrated souls, beings to be worshiped, p.

with such guests, have wisely refused them entry, the former permitting their approach to their shores but not their entry, while the latter permit this approach to only one European people, the Dutch, but treat them like prisoners, not allowing them any communication with the inhabitants. The worst of this (or, to speak with the moralist, the best) is that all these outrages profit them nothing, since all these commercial ventures stand on the verge of collapse, and the Sugar Islands, that place of the most refined and cruel slavery, produces no real revenue except indirectly, only serving a not very praiseworthy purpose of furnishing sailors for war fleets and thus for the conduct of war in Europe. This service is rendered to powers which make a great show of their piety, and, while they drink injustice like water, they regard themselves as the elect in point of orthodoxy.

Since the narrower or wider community of the peoples 360 of the earth has developed so far that a violation of rights in one place is felt throughout the world, the idea of a law of world citizenship is no high-flown or exaggerated notion. It is a supplement to the unwritten code of the civil and international law, indispensable for the maintenance of the public human rights and hence also of perpetual peace. One cannot flatter oneself into believing one can approach this peace except under the condition outlined here.

---

223). That mysterious expression *Konx Ompax* may well mean "the holy" (*Konx*), the blessed (*Om*), the wise (*Pax*), the supreme being pervading the world (nature personified). Its use in the Greek mysteries may indicate monotheism among the epopts in contrast to the polytheism of the people (though Orazio scented atheism there). How that mysterious word came to the Greeks via Tibet can perhaps be explained in this way; and the early traffic of Europe with China, also through Tibet, and perhaps earlier than communication with Hindustan, is made probable.

FIRST SUPPLEMENT

OF THE GUARANTEE FOR PERPETUAL PEACE

The guarantee of perpetual peace is nothing less than that great artist, nature (*natura daedala rerum*). In her mechanical course we see that her aim is to produce a harmony among men, against their will and indeed through
361   their discord. As a necessity working according to laws we do not know, we call it destiny. But, considering its design
362   in world history, we call it "providence," inasmuch as we discern in it the profound wisdom of a higher cause which predetermines the course of nature and directs it to the objective final end of the human race.[1] We do not observe or

[1] In the mechanism of nature, to which man belongs as a sensuous being, a form is exhibited which is basic to its existence; we can conceive of this form only as dependent upon the end to which the Author of the world has previously destined it. This predetermination we call "divine providence" generally, and so far as it is exercised at the beginning of the world we call it "founding providence" (*Providentia conditrix; semel iussit, semper parent*, Augustine).* As maintaining nature in its course by universal laws of design, it is called "ruling providence" (*providentia gubernatrix*); as directing nature to ends not foreseen by man and only conjectured from the actual result, it is called "guiding providence" (*providentia directrix*). With respect to single events as divine ends, it is no longer called "providence" but "dispensation" (*directio extraordinaria*). But since "divine dispensation" indicates miracles, even if the events themselves are not called such, it is a foolish pretension of man to wish to interpret them as such, since it is absurd to infer from a single event to a particular principle of the efficient cause, namely, that this event is an end and not merely a mechanical corollary of another end wholly unknown to us. However pious and humble such talk may be, it is full of self-conceit. The division of providence, considered not formally but materially, i.e., with respect to objects in the world to which it is directed, into either general or particular providence, is false and

* ["Providence is a founder; once she orders, they always obey."]

infer this providence in the cunning contrivances of nature, but, as in questions of the relation of the form of things to ends in general, we can and must supply it from our own minds in order to conceive of its possibility by analogy to actions of human art. The Idea of the relation-

---

self-contradictory. (This division appears, for instance, in the statement that providence cares for the preservation of the species but leaves individuals to chance.) It is contradictory because it is called universal in its purpose, and therefore no single thing can be excluded from it. Presumably, therefore, a formal distinction is intended, according to the way in which providence seeks its ends. This is the distinction between the ordinary and the special ways of providence. (Under the former we may cite the annual dying-out and rebirth of nature with the changes of the season; under the latter, the transport of wood by ocean currents to arctic lands where it cannot grow, yet where it is needed by the inhabitants who could not live without it.) Although we can very well explain the physico-mechanical cause of these extraordinary cases (e.g., by reference to the wooded banks of rivers in temperate lands, the falling of trees into the rivers, and then their being carried along by the Gulf Stream), we must not overlook the teleological cause, which intimates the foresight of a wisdom commanding over nature.

The concept of intervention or concurrence (*concursus*) in producing an effect in the world of sense must be given up, though it is quite usual in the schools. For to try to pair the disparate (*gryphes iungere equis*),† and to let that which is itself the perfect cause of events in the world supplement its own predetermining providence in the course of the world (which would therefore have to have been inadequate), is self-contradictory. We fall into this self-contradiction, for example, when we say that next to God it was the physician who cured the ill, as if God had been his helper. For *causa solitaria non iuvat;* God is the author of the physician and all his medicines, and if we insist on ascending to the highest but theoretically inconceivable first cause, the effect must be ascribed entirely to Him. Or we can ascribe it entirely to the physician, so far as we consider the occurrence as explicable in a chain of causes under the order of nature.

But, besides being self-contradictory, such a mode of thought brings an end to all definite principles in judging an effect. In a morally practical point of view, however, which is directed exclusively to the supersensuous, the concept of the divine *concursus* is quite suitable and even necessary. We find this, for instance, in the belief that God

362

† ["Griffins shall mate with mares." An allusion to Virgil, *Eclogue* VIII.]

ship and harmony between these actions and the end
which reason directly assigns to us is transcendent from a
theoretical point of view; from a practical standpoint, with
respect, for example, to the ideal of perpetual peace, the
concept is dogmatic and its reality is well established, and
thus the mechanism of nature may be employed to that
end. The use of the word "nature" is more fitting to the
limits of human reason and more modest than an expression indicating a providence unknown to us. This is especially true when we are dealing with questions of theory
and not of religion, as at present, for human reason in
questions of the relation of effects to their causes must remain within the limits of possible experience. On the other
hand, the use of the word "providence" here intimates the
possession of wings like those of Icarus, conducting us toward the secret of its unfathomable purpose.

Before we more narrowly define the guarantee which nature gives, it is necessary to examine the situation in which
she has placed her actors on her vast stage, a situation
which finally assures peace among them. Then we shall see
363 how she accomplishes the latter. Her preparatory arrange-
ments are:

1. In every region of the world she has made it possible
   for men to live.
2. By war she has driven them even into the most inhospitable regions in order to populate them.
3. By the same means, she has forced them into more or
   less lawful relations with each other.

That in the cold wastes by the Arctic Ocean the moss
grows which the reindeer digs from the snow in order to
_____
will compensate for our own lack of justice, provided our intention
was genuine; that He will do so by means that are inconceivable to
us, and that therefore we should not relent in our endeavor after the
good. But it is self-evident that no one should try to explain a good
action (as an event in the world) as a result of this *concursus*, for this
would be a vain theoretical knowledge of the supersensuous and
therefore absurd.

make itself the prey or the conveyance of the Ostyak or Samoyed; or that the saline sandy deserts are inhabited by the camel which appears created as it were in order that they might not go unused—that is already wonderful. Still clearer is the end when we see how besides the furry animals of the Arctic there are also the seal, the walrus, and the whale which afford the inhabitants food from their flesh and warmth from their blubber. But the care of nature excites the greatest wonder when we see how she brings wood (though the inhabitants do not know whence it comes) to these barren climates, without which they would have neither canoes, weapons, nor huts, and when we see how these natives are so occupied with their war against the animals that they live in peace with each other —but what drove them there was presumably nothing else than war.

The first instrument of war among the animals which man learned to tame and to domesticate was the horse (for the elephant belongs to later times, to the luxury of already established states). The art of cultivating certain types of plants (grain) whose original characteristics we do not know, and the increase and improvement of fruits by transplantation and grafting (in Europe perhaps only the crab apple and the wild pear), could arise only under conditions prevailing in already established states where property was secure. Before this could take place, it was necessary that men who had first subsisted in anarchic freedom by hunting,[2] fishing, and sheepherding should have been

2 Among all modes of life there is undoubtedly none more opposed to a civilized constitution than that of hunting, because families which must dwell separately soon become strangers and, scattered in extensive forests, also enemies, since each needs a great deal of space for obtaining food and clothing. The Noachic ban on blood (Genesis 9:4-6) (which was imposed by the baptized Jews as a condition on the later Christians who were converted from heathenism, though in a different connection—see The Acts 15:20; 21:25) seems to have been originally nothing more than a prohibition against the hunting life, because here raw flesh must often have been eaten; when the latter was forbidden, so also was the former.

364

364　forced into an agricultural life. Then salt and iron were
discovered. These were perhaps the first articles of commerce for the various peoples and were sought far and
wide; in this way a peaceful traffic among nations was established, and thus understanding, conventions, and peaceable relations were established among the most distant
peoples.

As nature saw to it that men *could* live everywhere in
the world, she also despotically willed that they *should* do
so, even against their inclination and without this *ought*
being based on a concept of duty to which they were
bound by a moral law. She chose war as the means to this
end. So we see peoples whose common language shows that
they have a common origin. For instance, the Samoyeds on
the Arctic Ocean and a people with a similar language a
thousand miles away in the Altaian Mountains are separated by a Mongolian people adept at horsemanship and
hence at war; the latter drove the former into the most inhospitable arctic regions where they certainly would not
have spread of their own accord.[3] Again, it is the same
with the Finns who in the most northerly part of Europe
are called Lapps; Goths and Sarmatians have separated
365　them from the Hungarians to whom they are related in
language. What can have driven the Eskimos, a race entirely distinct from all others in America and perhaps de-
scended from primeval European adventurers, so far into
the North, or the Pescherais as far south as Tierra del
Fuego, if it were not war which nature uses to populate
the whole earth? War itself requires no special motive but

[3] One could ask: If nature willed that these icy coasts should not
remain uninhabited, what would become of the inhabitants if nature
ever failed (as might be expected) to bring driftwood to them? For it
is reasonable to believe that, in the progress of civilization, the occu-
pants of the temperate zone would make better use of the wood along
rivers than simply to let it fall into the water and be carried to the
sea. I answer: If nature compels them to peace, the dwellers along the
Ob, the Yenisei, or the Lena will bring it to them, exchanging it for
animal products in which the sea around the Arctic coasts abounds.

appears to be engrafted on human nature; it passes even for something noble, to which the love of glory impels men quite apart from any selfish urges. Thus among the American savages, just as much as among those of Europe during the age of chivalry, military valor is held to be of great worth in itself, not only during war (which is natural) but in order that there should be war. Often war is waged only in order to show valor; thus an inner dignity is ascribed to war itself, and even some philosophers have praised it as an ennoblement of humanity, forgetting the pronouncement of the Greek who said, "War is an evil inasmuch as it produces more wicked men than it takes away." So much for the measures nature takes to lead the human race, considered as a class of animals, to her own end.

Now we come to the question concerning that which is most essential in the design of perpetual peace: What has nature done with regard to this end which man's own reason makes his duty? That is, what has nature done to favor man's moral purpose, and how has she guaranteed (by compulsion but without prejudice to his freedom) that he shall do that which he ought to but does not do under the laws of freedom? This question refers to all three phases of public law, namely, civil law, the law of nations, and the law of world citizenship. If I say of nature that she wills that this or that occur, I do not mean that she imposes a duty on us to do it, for this can be done only by free practical reason; rather I mean that she herself does it, whether we will or not (*fata volentem ducunt, nolentem trahunt*).[4]

1. Even if a people were not forced by internal discord to submit to public laws, war would compel them to do so, for we have already seen that nature has placed each people near another which presses upon it, and against this it must form itself into a state in order to defend itself. Now the republican constitution is the only one entirely fitting to the rights of man. But it is the most difficult to estab-

366

4 ["Fates lead the willing, drive the unwilling" (Seneca, *Epist. mor.* XVIII. 4).]

lish and even harder to preserve, so that many[5] say a republic would have to be a nation of angels, because men with their selfish inclinations are not capable of a constitution of such sublime form. But precisely with these inclinations nature comes to the aid of the general will established on reason, which is revered even though impotent in practice. Thus it is only a question of a good organization of the state (which does lie in man's power), whereby the powers of each selfish inclination are so arranged in opposition that one moderates or destroys the ruinous effect of the other. The consequence for reason is the same as if none of them existed, and man is forced to be a good citizen even if not a morally good person.

The problem of organizing a state, however hard it may seem, can be solved even for a race of devils, if only they are intelligent. The problem is: "Given a multitude of rational beings requiring universal laws for their preservation, but each of whom is secretly inclined to exempt himself from them, to establish a constitution in such a way that, although their private intentions conflict, they check each other, with the result that their public conduct is the same as if they had no such intentions."

A problem like this must be capable of solution; it does not require that we know how to attain the moral improvement of men but only that we should know the mechanism of nature in order to use it on men, organizing the conflict of the hostile intentions present in a people in such a way that they must compel themselves to submit to coercive laws. Thus a state of peace is established in which laws have force. We can see, even in actual states, which are far from perfectly organized, that in their foreign relations they approach that which the idea of right prescribes. This is so in spite of the fact that the intrinsic element of morality is certainly not the cause of it. (A good constitution is not to be expected from morality, but, conversely, a

[5] [E.g., Rousseau, *Social Contract*. Book III, chap. 4.]

good moral condition of a people is to be expected only under a good constitution.) Instead of genuine morality, the mechanism of nature brings it to pass through selfish inclinations, which naturally conflict outwardly but which can be used by reason as a means for its own end, the   367 sovereignty of law, and, as concerns the state, for promoting and securing internal and external peace.

This, then, is the truth of the matter: Nature inexorably wills that the right should finally triumph. What we neglect to do comes about by itself, though with great inconveniences to us. "If you bend the reed too much, you break it; and he who attempts too much attempts nothing" (Bouterwek).[6]

2. The idea of international law presupposes the separate existence of many independent but neighboring states. Although this condition is itself a state of war (unless a federative union prevents the outbreak of hostilities), this is rationally preferable to the amalgamation of states under one superior power, as this would end in one universal monarchy, and laws always lose in vigor what government gains in extent; hence a soulless despotism falls into anarchy after stifling the seeds of the good. Nevertheless, every state, or its ruler, desires to establish lasting peace in this way, aspiring if possible to rule the whole world. But nature wills otherwise. She employs two means to separate peoples and to prevent them from mixing: differences of language and of religion.[7] These differences involve a tendency to mutual hatred and pretexts for war, but the prog-

6 [Friedrich Bouterwek (1766-1828).]

7 Difference of religion—a singular expression! It is precisely as if one spoke of different moralities. There may very well be different kinds of historical faiths attached to different means employed in the promotion of religion, and they belong merely in the field of learned investigation. Similarly there may be different religious texts (Zenda-vesta, the Veda, the Koran, etc.), but such differences do not exist in religion, there being only one religion valid for all men and in all ages. These can, therefore, be nothing else than accidental vehicles of religion, thus changing with times and places.

ress of civilization and men's gradual approach to greater harmony in their principles finally leads to peaceful agreement. This is not like that peace which despotism (in the burial ground of freedom) produces through a weakening of all powers; it is, on the contrary, produced and maintained by their equilibrium in liveliest competition.

368   3. Just as nature wisely separates nations, which the will of every state, sanctioned by the principles of international law, would gladly unite by artifice or force, nations which could not have secured themselves against violence and war by means of the law of world citizenship unite because of mutual interest. The spirit of commerce, which is incompatible with war, sooner or later gains the upper hand in every state. As the power of money is perhaps the most dependable of all the powers (means) included under the state power, states see themselves forced, without any moral urge, to promote honorable peace and by mediation to prevent war wherever it threatens to break out. They do so exactly as if they stood in perpetual alliances, for great offensive alliances are in the nature of the case rare and even less often successful.

In this manner nature guarantees perpetual peace by the mechanism of human passions. Certainly she does not do so with sufficient certainty for us to predict the future in any theoretical sense, but adequately from a practical point of view, making it our duty to work toward this end, which is not just a chimerical one.

SECOND SUPPLEMENT

SECRET ARTICLE FOR PERPETUAL PEACE

A secret article in contracts under public law is objectively, i.e., from the standpoint of its content, a contradiction. Subjectively, however, a secret clause can be present in them, because the persons who dictate it might find it compromising to their dignity to declare openly that they are its authors.

The only article of this kind is contained in the statement: "The opinions of philosophers on the conditions of the possibility of public peace shall be consulted by those states armed for war."

But it appears humiliating to the legislative authority of a state, to whom we must naturally attribute the utmost wisdom, to seek instruction from subjects (the philosophers) on principles of conduct toward other states. It is nevertheless very advisable to do so. Therefore, the state 369 tacitly and secretly invites them to give their opinions, that is, the state will let them publicly and freely talk about the general maxims of warfare and of the establishment of peace (for they will do that of themselves, provided they are not forbidden to do so). It does not require a particular convention among states to see that this is done, since their agreement on this point lies in an obligation already established by universal human reason which is morally legislative.

I do not mean that the state should give the principles of philosophers any preference over the decisions of lawyers (the representatives of the state power); I only ask that they be given a hearing. The lawyer, who has made not only the scales of right but also the sword of justice his symbol, generally uses the latter not merely to keep back all foreign influences from the former, but, if the scale does not sink the way he wishes, he also throws the sword into it (*vae victis*), a practice to which he often has the greatest temptation because he is not also a philosopher, even in morality. His office is only to apply positive laws, not to inquire whether they might not need improvement. The administrative function, which is the lower one in his faculty, he counts as the higher because it is invested with power (as is the case also with the other faculties [of medicine and theology]).[1] The philosophical faculty occupies a very low rank against this allied power. Thus it is said of philosophy, for example, that she is the handmaiden to theology, and the other faculties claim as much. But one does not see distinctly whether she precedes her mistress with a flambeau or follows bearing her train.

That kings should philosophize or philosophers become kings is not to be expected. Nor is it to be wished, since the possession of power inevitably corrupts the untrammeled judgment of reason. But kings or kinglike peoples which rule themselves under laws of equality should not suffer the class of philosophers to disappear or to be silent, but should let them speak openly. This is indispensable to the enlightenment of the business of government, and, since the class of philosophers is by nature incapable of plotting and lobbying, it is above suspicion of being made up of propagandists.

[1] [Cf. Introduction, p. xi, note 5.]

APPENDIX I

ON THE OPPOSITION BETWEEN MORAL-
ITY AND POLITICS WITH RESPECT
TO PERPETUAL PEACE

Taken objectively, morality is in itself practical, being   370
the totality of unconditionally mandatory laws according
to which we ought to act. It would obviously be absurd,
after granting authority to the concept of duty, to pretend
that we cannot do our duty, for in that case this concept
would itself drop out of morality (*ultra posse nemo obli-
gatur*). Consequently, there can be no conflict of politics,
as a practical doctrine of right, with ethics, as a theoretical
doctrine of right. That is to say, there is no conflict of
practice with theory, unless by ethics we mean a general
doctrine of prudence, which would be the same as a theory
of the maxims for choosing the most fitting means to accomplish the purposes of self-interest. But to give this
meaning to ethics is equivalent to denying that there is
any such thing at all.

Politics says, "Be ye wise as serpents"; morality adds, as
a limiting condition, "and guileless as doves." If these two
injunctions are incompatible in a single command, then
politics and morality are really in conflict; but if these two
qualities ought always to be united, the thought of con-
trariety is absurd, and the question as to how the conflict
between morals and politics is to be resolved cannot even
be posed as a problem. Although the proposition, "Honesty is the best policy," implies a theory which practice un-
fortunately often refutes, the equally theoretical "Honesty
is better than any policy" is beyond refutation and is indeed the indispensable condition of policy.

The tutelary divinity of morality yields not to Jupiter,

for this tutelary divinity of force still is subject to destiny. That is, reason is not yet sufficiently enlightened to survey the entire series of predetermining causes, and such vision would be necessary for one to be able to foresee with certainty the happy or unhappy effects which follow human actions by the mechanism of nature (though we know enough to have hope that they will accord with our wishes). But what we have to do in order to remain in the path of duty (according to rules of wisdom) reason instructs us by her rules, and her teaching suffices for attaining the ultimate end.

371   Now the practical man, to whom morality is mere theory even though he concedes that it can and should be followed, ruthlessly renounces our fond hope [that it will be followed]. He does so because he pretends to have seen in advance that man, by his nature, will never will what is required for realizing the goal of perpetual peace. Certainly the will of each individual to live under a juridical constitution according to principles of freedom (i.e., the distributive unity of the will of all) is not sufficient to this end. That all together should will this condition (i.e., the collective unity of the united will)—the solution to this troublous problem—is also required. Thus a whole of civil society is formed. But since a uniting cause must supervene upon the variety of particular volitions in order to produce a common will from them, establishing this whole is something no one individual in the group can perform; hence in the practical execution of this idea we can count on nothing but force to establish the juridical condition, on the compulsion of which public law will later be established. We can scarcely hope to find in the legislator a moral intention sufficient to induce him to commit to the general will the establishment of a legal constitution after he has formed the nation from a horde of savages; therefore, we cannot but expect (in practice) to find in execution wide deviations from this idea (in theory).

It will then be said that he who once has power in his

hands will not allow the people to prescribe laws for him; a state which once is able to stand under no external laws will not submit to the decision of other states how it should seek its rights against them; and one continent, which feels itself superior to another, even though the other does not interfere with it, will not neglect to increase its power by robbery or even conquest. Thus all theoretical plans of civil and international laws and laws of world citizenship vanish into empty and impractical ideas, while practice based on empirical principles of human nature, not blushing to draw its maxims from the usages of the world, can alone hope to find a sure ground for its political edifice.

If there is no freedom and no morality based on free- 372 dom, and everything which occurs or can occur happens by the mere mechanism of nature, certainly politics (which is the art of using this mechanism for ruling men) is the whole of practical wisdom, and the concept of right is an empty thought. But if we find it necessary to connect the latter with politics, and even to raise it to a limiting condition thereon, the possibility of their being united must be conceded. I can easily conceive of a moral politician, i.e., one who so chooses political principles that they are consistent with those of morality; but I cannot conceive of a political moralist, one who forges a morality in such a way that it conforms to the statesman's advantage.

When a remediable defect is found in the constitution of the state or in its relations to others, the principle of the moral politician will be that it is a duty, especially of the rulers of the state, to inquire how it can be remedied as soon as possible in a way conforming to natural law as a model presented by reason; this he will do even if it costs self-sacrifice. But it would be absurd to demand that every defect be immediately and impetuously changed, since the disruption of the bonds of a civil society or a union of world citizens before a better constitution is ready to take its place is against all politics agreeing with morality. But it can be demanded that at least the maxim of the necessity of such a change should be taken to heart by those in power, so that they may continuously approach the goal of the constitution that is best under laws of right. A state may exercise a republican rule, even though by its present constitution it has a despotic sovereignty, until gradually the people becomes susceptible to the influence simply of the idea of the authority of law (as if it possessed physical power) and thus is found fit to be its own legislator (as its own legislation is originally established on law). If a violent revolution, engendered by a bad constitution, introduces by illegal means a more legal constitution, to lead the people back to the earlier constitution would not be permitted; but, while the revolution lasted, each person who openly or covertly shared in it would have justly in-

373 curred the punishment due to those who rebel. As to the external relations of states, a state cannot be expected to renounce its constitution even though it is a despotic one (which has the advantage of being stronger in relation to foreign enemies) so long as it is exposed to the danger of being swallowed up by other states. Thus even in the case of the intention to improve the constitution, postponement to a more propitious time may be permitted.[1]

It may be that despotizing moralists, in practice blundering, often violate rules of political prudence through measures they adopt or propose too precipitately; but experi-

---

[1] These are permissive laws of reason. Public law laden with injustice must be allowed to stand, either until everything is of itself ripe for complete reform or until this maturity has been brought about by peaceable means; for a legal constitution, even though it be right to only a low degree, is better than none at all, the anarchic condition which would result from precipitate reform. Political wisdom, therefore, will make it a duty to introduce reforms which accord with the ideal of public law. But even when nature herself produces revolutions, political wisdom will not employ them to legitimize still greater oppression. On the contrary, it will use them as a call of nature for fundamental reforms to produce a lawful constitution founded upon principles of freedom, for only such a constitution is durable.

ence will gradually retrieve them from their infringement of nature and lead them on to a better course. But the moralizing politician, by glossing over principles of politics which are opposed to the right with the pretext that human nature is not capable of the good as reason prescribes it, only makes reform impossible and perpetuates the violation of law.

Instead of possessing the *practical science* they boast of, these politicians have only *practices;* they flatter the power which is then ruling so as not to be remiss in their private advantage, and they sacrifice the nation and, possibly, the whole world. This is the way of all professional lawyers (not legislators) when they go into politics. Their task is not to reason too nicely about the legislation but to execute the momentary commands on the statute books; consequently, the legal constitution in force at any time is to them the best, but when it is amended from above, this amendment always seems best, too. Thus everything is preserved in its accustomed mechanical order. Their adroitness in fitting into all circumstances gives them the illusion 374 of being able to judge constitutional principles according to concepts of right (not empirically, but a priori). They make a great show of understanding *men* (which is certainly something to be expected of them, since they have to deal with so many) without understanding *man* and what can be made of him, for they lack the higher point of view of anthropological observation which is needed for this. If with these ideas they go into civil and international law, as reason prescribes it, they take this step in a spirit of chicanery, for they still follow their accustomed mechanical routine of despotically imposed coercive laws in a field where only concepts of reason can establish a legal compulsion according to the principles of freedom, under which alone a just and durable constitution is possible. In this field the pretended practical man thinks he can solve the problem of establishing such a constitution without the rational Idea but solely from the experience he has had with what was previously the most lasting constitution—a constitution which in many cases was opposed to the right.

The maxims which he makes use of (though he does not divulge them) are, roughly speaking, the following sophisms:

1. *Fac et excusa.* Seize every favorable opportunity for usurping the right of the state over its own people or over a neighboring people; the justification will be easier and more elegant *ex post facto,* and the power can be more easily glossed over, especially when the supreme power in the state is also the legislative authority which must be obeyed without argument. It is much more difficult to do the violence when one has first to wait upon the consideration of convincing arguments and to meet them with counterarguments. Boldness itself gives the appearance of inner conviction of the legitimacy of the deed, and the god of success is afterward the best advocate.

2. *Si fecisti, nega.* What you have committed, deny that it was your fault—for instance, that you have brought your people to despair and hence to rebellion. Rather assert that it was due to the obstinacy of your subjects; or, if you have conquered a neighboring nation, say that the fault 375 lies in the nature of man, who, if not met by force, can be counted on to make use of it to conquer you.

3. *Divide et impera.* That is, if there are certain privileged persons in your nation who have chosen you as their chief (*primus inter pares*), set them at variance with one another and embroil them with the people. Show the latter visions of greater freedom, and all will soon depend on your untrammeled will. Or if it is foreign states that concern you, it is a pretty safe means to sow discord among them so that, by seeming to protect the weaker, you can conquer them one after another.

Certainly no one is now the dupe of these political maxims, for they are already universally known. Nor are they blushed at, as if their injustice were too glaring, for great powers blush only at the judgment of other great powers but not at that of the common masses. It is not that they are ashamed of revealing such principles (for all of them are in the same boat with respect to the morality of their maxims); they are ashamed only when these maxims fail, for they still have political honor which cannot be disputed—and this honor is the aggrandizement of their power by whatever means.[2]

All these twistings and turnings of an immoral doctrine of prudence in leading men from their natural state of war to a state of peace prove at least that men in both their private and their public relationships cannot reject the concept of right or trust themselves openly to establish politics merely on the artifices of prudence. Thus they do not refuse obedience to the concept of public law, which is especially manifest in international law; on the contrary,

376

[2] Even if we doubt a certain wickedness in the nature of men who live together in a state, and instead plausibly cite lack of civilization, which is not yet sufficiently advanced, i.e., regard barbarism as the cause of those antilawful manifestations of their character, this viciousness is clearly and incontestably shown in the foreign relations of states. Within each state it is veiled by the compulsion of civil laws, because the inclination to violence between the citizens is fettered by the stronger power of the government. This relationship not only gives a moral veneer (*causae non causae*) to the whole but actually facilitates the development of the moral disposition to a direct respect for the law by placing a barrier against the outbreak of unlawful inclinations. Each person believes that he himself would hold the concept of law sacred and faithfully follow it provided he were sure that he could expect the same from others, and the government does in part assure him of this. Thereby a great step (though not yet a moral step) is taken toward morality, which is attachment to this concept of duty for its own sake and without regard to hope of a similar response from others. But since each one with his own good opinion of himself presupposes a malicious disposition on the part of all the others, they all pronounce the judgment that they in fact are all worth very little. We shall not discuss how this comes about, though it cannot be blamed on the nature of man as a free being. But since even respect for the concept of right (which man cannot absolutely refuse to respect) solemnly sanctions the theory that he has the capacity of conforming to it, everyone sees that he, for his part, must act according to it, however others may act.

376

they give all due honor to it, even when they are inventing a hundred pretenses and subterfuges to escape from it in practice, imputing its authority, as the source and union of all laws, to crafty force.

Let us put an end to this sophism, if not to the injustice it protects, and force the false representatives of power to confess that they do not plead in favor of the right but in favor of might. This is revealed in the imperious tone they assume as if they themselves could command the right. Let us remove the delusion by which they and others are duped, and discover the supreme principle from which the intention to perpetual peace stems. Let us show that everything evil which stands in its way derives from the fact that the political moralist begins where the moral politician would correctly leave off, and that, since he thus subordinates principles to the end (putting the cart before the horse), he vitiates his own purpose of bringing politics into agreement with morality.

To make practical philosophy self-consistent, it is necessary, first, to decide the question: In problems of practical reason, must we begin from its material principles, i.e., the end as the object of choice? Or should we begin from the formal principles of pure reason, i.e., from the principle which is concerned solely with freedom in outer relations and which reads, "So act that you can will that your maxim could become a universal law, regardless of the end"?

Without doubt it is the latter which has precedence, for as a principle of law it has unconditional necessity. On the other hand, the former is obligatory only if we presuppose the empirical conditions of the proposed end, i.e., its practicability. Thus if this end (in this case, perpetual peace) is a duty, it must be derived from the formal principle of the maxims of external actions. The first principle, that of the political moralist, pertaining to civil and international law and the law of world citizenship, is merely a problem of technique (*problema technicum*); the second, as the prob-

377

lem of the moral politician to whom it is an ethical problem (*problema morale*), is far removed from the other in its method of leading toward perpetual peace, which is wished not merely as a material good but also as a condition issuing from an acknowledgment of duty.

For the solution of the former, the problem of political prudence, much knowledge of nature is required so that its mechanism may be employed toward the desired end; yet all this is uncertain in its results for perpetual peace, with whatever sphere of public law we are concerned. It is uncertain, for example, whether the people are better kept in obedience and maintained in prosperity by severity or by the charm of distinctions which flatter their vanity, by the power of one or the union of various chiefs, or perhaps merely by a serving nobility or by the power of the people. History furnishes us with contradictory examples from all governments (with the exception of the truly republican, which can alone appeal to the mind of a moral politician). Still more uncertain is an international law allegedly erected on the statutes of ministries. It is, in fact, a word without meaning, resting as it does on compacts which, in the very act of being concluded, contain secret reservations for their violation.

On the other hand, the solution of the second problem, that of political wisdom, presses itself upon us, as it were; it is clear to everyone and puts to shame all affectation. It leads directly to the end, but, remembering discretion, it 378 does not precipitately hasten to do so by force; rather, it continuously approaches it under the conditions offered by favorable circumstances.

Then it may be said, "Seek ye first the kingdom of pure practical reason and its righteousness, and your end (the blessing of perpetual peace) will necessarily follow." For it is the peculiarity of morals, especially with respect to its principles of public law and hence in relation to a politics known a priori, that the less it makes conduct depend on the proposed end, i.e., the intended material or moral ad-

vantage, the more it agrees with it in general. This is because it is the universal will given a priori (in a nation or
in the relations among different nations) which determines
the law among men, and if practice consistently follows it,
this will can also, by the mechanism of nature, cause the
desired result and make the concept of law effective. So,
for instance, it is a principle of moral politics that a people
should unite into a state according to juridical concepts of
freedom and equality, and this principle is based not on
prudence but on duty. Political moralists may argue as
much as they wish about the natural mechanism of a mass
of men forming a society, assuming a mechanism which
would weaken those principles and vitiate their end; or
they may seek to prove their assertions by examples of
poorly organized constitutions of ancient and modern times
(for instance, of democracies without representative systems). They deserve no hearing, particularly as such a per-
nicious theory may itself occasion the evil which it prophe-
sies, throwing human beings into one class with all other
living machines, differing from them only in their consciousness that they are not free, which makes them, in
their own judgment, the most miserable of all beings in
the world.

The true but somewhat boastful sentence which has become proverbial, *Fiat iustitia, pereat mundus* ("Let justice
reign even if all the rascals in the world should perish from
it"), is a stout principle of right which cuts asunder the
379 whole tissue of artifice or force. But it should not be mis-
understood as a permission to use one's own right with extreme rigor (which would conflict with ethical duty); it
should be understood as the obligation of those in power
not to limit or to extend anyone's right through sympathy
or disfavor. This requires, first, an internal constitution of
the state erected on pure principles of right, and, second, a
convention of the state with other near or distant states
(analogous to a universal state) for the legal settlement of
their differences. This implies only that political maxims

must not be derived from the welfare or happiness which a single state expects from obedience to them, and thus not from the end which one of them proposes for itself. That is, they must not be deduced from volition as the supreme yet empirical principle of political wisdom, but rather from the pure concept of the duty of right, from the *ought* whose principle is given a priori by pure reason, regardless of what the physical consequences may be. The world will by no means perish by a diminution in the number of evil men. Moral evil has the indiscerptible property of being opposed to and destructive of its own purposes (especially in the relationships between evil men); thus it gives place to the moral principle of the good, though only through a slow progress.

Thus objectively, or in theory, there is no conflict between morals and politics. Subjectively, however, in the selfish propensity of men (which should not be called "practice," as this would imply that it rested on rational maxims), this conflict will always remain. Indeed, it should remain, because it serves as a whetstone of virtue, whose true courage (by the principle, *tu ne cede malis, sed contra audentior ito*) [3] in the present case does not so much consist in defying with strong resolve evils and sacrifices which must be undertaken along with the conflict, but rather in detecting and conquering the crafty and far more dangerously deceitful and treasonable principle of evil in ourselves, which puts forward the weakness of human nature as justification for every transgression.

In fact, the political moralist may say: The ruler and 380 people, or nation and nation, do each other no injustice when by violence or fraud they make war on each other, although they do commit injustice in general in that they refuse to respect the concept of right, which alone could establish perpetual peace. For since the one does transgress his duty against the other, who is likewise lawlessly disposed toward him, each gets what he deserves, when they

[3] ["Yield not to evils, but go against the stronger" (*Aeneid* VI. 95).]

destroy each other. But enough of the race still remains to let this game continue into the remotest ages in order that posterity, some day, might take these perpetrators as a warning example. Hence providence is justified in the history of the world, for the moral principle in man is never extinguished, while with advancing civilization reason grows pragmatically in its capacity to realize ideas of law. But at the same time the culpability for the transgressions also grows. If we assume that humanity never will or can be improved, the only thing which a theodicy seems unable to justify is creation itself, the fact that a race of such corrupt beings ever was on earth. But the point of view necessary for such an assumption is far too high for us, and we cannot theoretically support our philosophical concepts of the supreme power which is inscrutable to us.

To such dubious consequences we are inevitably driven if we do not assume that pure principles of right have objective reality, i.e., that they may be applied, and that the people in a state and, further, states themselves in their mutual relations should act according to them, whatever objections empirical politics may raise. Thus true politics can never take a step without rendering homage to morality. Though politics by itself is a difficult art, its union with morality is no art at all, for this union cuts the knot which politics could not untie when they were in conflict. The rights of men must be held sacred, however much sacrifice it may cost the ruling power. One cannot compromise here and seek the middle course of a pragmatic conditional law between the morally right and the expedient. All politics must bend its knee before the right. But by this it can hope slowly to reach the stage where it will shine with an immortal glory.

APPENDIX II

OF THE HARMONY WHICH THE TRAN-SCENDENTAL CONCEPT OF PUBLIC RIGHT ESTABLISHES BETWEEN MORALITY AND POLITICS

If, like the teacher of law, I abstract from all the mate- 381
rial of public law (i.e., abstract from the various empirically given relationships of men in the state or of states to
each other), there remains only the *form* of publicity, the
possibility of which is implied by every legal claim, since
without it there can be no justice (which can only be conceived as publicly known) and thus no right, since it can
be conferred only in accordance with justice. Every legal
claim must be capable of publicity. Since it is easy to judge
whether it is so in a particular case, i.e., whether it can be
compatible with the principles of the agent, this gives an
easily applied criterion found a priori in reason, by which
the falsity (opposition to law) of the pretended claim (*prae-
tensio iuris*) can, as it were, be immediately known by an
experiment of pure reason.

Having set aside everything empirical in the concept of
civil or international law (such as the wickedness in human nature which necessitates coercion), we can call the
following proposition the transcendental formula of public
law: "All actions relating to the right of other men are unjust if their maxim is not consistent with publicity."

This principle is to be regarded not merely as ethical (as
belonging to the doctrine of virtue) but also as juridical
(concerning the right of man). A maxim which I cannot
divulge without defeating my own purpose must be kept
secret if it is to succeed; and, if I cannot publicly avow it
without inevitably exciting universal opposition to my

project, the necessary and universal opposition which can
be foreseen a priori is due only to the injustice with which
the maxim threatens everyone. This principle is, furthermore, only negative, i.e., it only serves for the recognition
of what is not just to others. Like an axiom, it is indemon-
382 strably certain and, as will be seen in the following examples of public law, easily applied.

1. In the law of the state (*ius civitatis*) or domestic law,
there is a question which many hold to be difficult to answer, yet it is easily solved by the transcendental principle
of publicity. The question is: "Is rebellion a legitimate
means for a people to employ in throwing off the yoke of
an alleged tyrant (*non titulo, sed exercitio talis*)?" The
rights of the people are injured; no injustice befalls the
tyrant when he is deposed. There can be no doubt on this
point. Nevertheless, it is in the highest degree illegitimate
for the subjects to seek their rights in this way. If they fail
in the struggle and are then subjected to severest punishment, they cannot complain about injustice any more than
the tyrant could if they had succeeded.

If one wishes to decide this question by a dogmatic de-
duction of legal grounds, there can be much arguing pro
and con; only the transcendental principle of the publicity
of public law can free us of this prolixity. According to
this principle, a people would ask itself before the establishment of the civil contract whether it dare publish the
maxim of its intention to revolt on occasion. It is clear that
if, in the establishment of a constitution, the condition is
made that the people may in certain cases employ force
against its chief, the people would have to pretend to a
legitimate power over him, and then he would not be the
chief. Or if both are made the condition of the establishment of the state, no state would be possible, though to
establish it was the purpose of the people. The illegitimacy
of rebellion is thus clear from the fact that its maxim, if
openly acknowledged, would make its own purpose impossible. Therefore, it would have to be kept secret.

This secrecy, however, is not incumbent upon the chief of the state. He can openly say that he will punish every rebellion with the death of the ringleaders, however much they may believe that he was the first to overstep the basic law; for when he knows he possesses irresistible power (which must be assumed to be the case in every civil constitution, because he who does not have enough power to protect the people against every other also does not have the right to command them), he need not fear vitiating his own purpose by publishing his maxims. If the revolt of the people succeeds, what has been said is still quite compatible with the fact that the chief, on retiring to the status of a subject, cannot begin a revolt for his restoration but need not fear being made to account for his earlier administration of the state.

2. We can speak of international law only under the presupposition of some law-governed condition, i.e., of the external condition under which right can really be awarded to man. For, being a public law, it contains in its very concept the public announcement of a general will which assigns to each his rights, and this *status iuridicus* must result from some compact which is not founded on laws of compulsion (as in the case of the compact from which a single state arises). Rather, it must be founded on a free and enduring association, like the previously mentioned federation of states. For without there being some juridical condition, which actively binds together the different physical or moral persons, there can be only private law; this is the situation met with in the state of nature. Now here there is a conflict of politics with morality (regarding the latter as a science of right), and the criterion of publicity again finds an easy application in resolving it, though only if the compact between the states has been made with the purpose of preserving peace between them and other states, and not for conquest. The following cases of the antinomy between politics and morality occur (and they are stated with their solution).

383

a) "If one of these states has promised something to the other, such as aid, cession of some province, subsidies, and the like, and a case arises where the salvation of the state depends upon its being relieved of its promise, can it then consider itself in two roles: first as a sovereign (as it is responsible to no one in the state), and second as merely the highest official (who must give an account to the state)? From this dual capacity it would follow that in its latter role the state can relieve itself of what it has obliged itself to do in its former role." But if a state (or its chief) publi-

384   cizes this maxim, others would naturally avoid entering an alliance with it, or ally themselves with others so as to resist such pretensions. This proves that politics with all its cunning would defeat its purpose by candor; therefore, that maxim must be illegitimate.

b) "If a neighboring power becomes formidable by its acquisitions (*potentia tremenda*), and thus causes anxiety, can one assume because it *can* oppress that it *will?* And does this give the lesser power, in union with others, a right to attack it without having first been injured by it?" A state which made known that such was its maxim would produce the feared evil even more certainly and quickly, for the greater power would steal a march on the smaller. And the alliance of the smaller powers would be only a feeble reed against one who knew how to apply the maxim *divide et impera.* This maxim of political expediency, if made public, would necessarily defeat its own purpose, and hence it is illegitimate.

c) "If a smaller state is so situated as to break up the territory of a larger one, and continuous territory is necessary to the preservation of the larger, is the latter not justified in subjugating the smaller and incorporating it?" We easily see that the greater power cannot afford to let this maxim become known; otherwise the smaller states would very early unite, or other powers would dispute the prey, and thus publicity would render this maxim impracticable. This is a sign that it is illegitimate. It may be unjust to a very high degree, for a small object of injustice does not prevent the injustice from being very great.

3. I say nothing about the law of world citizenship, for its analogy with international law makes it a very simple matter to state and evaluate its maxims.

Thus in the principle of incompatibility between the maxims of international law and publicity we have a good distinguishing mark for recognizing the nonconformity of politics to morality (as a science of right). Now we need to know the condition under which these maxims agree with the law of nations, for we cannot infer conversely that the 385 maxims which bear publicity are therefore just, since no one who has decidedly superior power needs to conceal his plans. The condition of the possibility of international law in general is this: a juridical condition must first exist. For without this there is no public law, since all law which one may think of outside of this, in the state of nature, is merely private law. We have seen that a federation of states which has for its sole purpose the maintenance of peace is the only juridical condition compatible with the freedom of the several states. Therefore the harmony of politics with morals is possible only in a federative alliance, and the latter is necessary and given a priori by the principle of right. Furthermore, all politics has for its juridical basis the establishment of this harmony to its greatest possible extent, and without this end all its sophisms are but folly and veiled injustice. This false politics outdoes the best Jesuit school in casuistry. It has *reservatio mentalis,* wording public compacts with such expressions as can on occasion be interpreted to one's own advantage (for example, it makes the distinction between *status quo de fait* and *de droit*). It has *probabilism,* attributing hostile intentions to others, or even making probabilities of their possible superior power into legal grounds for destroying other, peaceful states. Finally, it has the *peccatum philosophicum (peccatillum, bagatelle),* holding it to be only a trifle when a small state is swallowed up in order that a much larger one may thereby approach more nearly to an alleged greater good for the world as a whole.[1]

The duplicity of politics in respect to morality, in using first one branch of it and then the other for its purposes, furthers these sophistic maxims. These branches are philanthropy and respect for the rights of men; and both are duty. The former is a conditional duty, while the latter is an unconditional and absolutely mandatory duty. One who wishes to give himself up to the sweet feeling of benevolence must make sure that he has not transgressed this absolute duty. Politics readily agrees with morality in its first branch (as ethics) in order to surrender the rights of men to their superiors. But with morality in the second branch (as a science of right), to which it must bend its knee, politics finds it advisable not to have any dealings, and rather denies it all reality, preferring to reduce all duties to mere benevolence. This artifice of a secretive politics would soon be unmasked by philosophy through publication of its maxims, if they only dared to allow the philosopher to publish his maxims.

In this regard I propose another affirmative and transcendental principle of public law, the formula of which is:

"All maxims which *stand in need* of publicity in order not to fail their end, agree with politics and right combined."

For if they can attain their end only through publicity, they must accord with the public's universal end, happi-

[1] The precedents for such maxims may be seen in Counselor Garve's treatise, *On the Union of Morality with Politics* (1788).* This worthy scholar admits in the beginning that he is not able to solve the problem completely. But to approve of this union while admitting that one cannot meet all objections which may be raised against it seems to show more tolerance than is advisable toward those who are inclined to abuse it.

* [Christian Garve (1742-98), *Abhandlung über die Verbindung der Moral mit der Politik oder einige Betrachtungen über die Frage, inwiefern es möglich sei, die Moral des Privatlebens bei der Regierung der Staaten zu beobachten* (Breslau, 1788).]

ness; and the proper task of politics is to promote this, i.e., to make the public satisfied with its condition. If, however, this end is attainable only by means of publicity, i.e., by removing all distrust in the maxims of politics, the latter must conform to the rights of the public, for only in this is the union of the goals of all possible.

The further development and discussion of this principle I must postpone to another occasion. But that it is a transcendental formula is to be seen from the exclusion of all empirical conditions (of the doctrine of happiness) as material of the law, and from the reference it makes to the form of universal lawfulness.

If it is a duty to make real (even if only through approximation in endless progress) the state of public law, and if there is well-grounded hope that this can actually be done, then perpetual peace, as the condition that will follow what has erroneously been called "treaties of peace" (but which in reality are only armistices), is not an empty idea. As the times required for equal steps of progress become, we hope, shorter and shorter, perpetual peace is a problem which, gradually working out its own solution, steadily approaches its goal.

AN OLD QUESTION RAISED AGAIN: IS THE HUMAN RACE CONSTANTLY PROGRESSING?[1]

1. WHAT DO WE *WANT* TO KNOW IN THIS MATTER?

We desire a fragment of human history and one, indeed, 79
that is drawn not from past but future time, therefore a predictive history; if it is not based on known laws (like eclipses of the sun and moon), this history is designated as divinatory, and yet natural; but if it can be acquired in no other way than through a supernatural communication and widening of one's view of future time, this history is called premonitory (prophetic).[2] If it is asked whether the human race at large is progressing perpetually toward the better, the important thing is not the natural history of man (whether new races may arise in the future), but rather his moral history and, more precisely, his history not as a species according to the generic notion (*singulorum*), but as the totality of men united socially on earth and apportioned into peoples (*universorum*).

2. HOW *CAN* WE KNOW IT?

As a divinatory historical narrative of things imminent in future time, consequently as a possible representation a priori of events which are supposed to happen then. But how is a history a priori possible? Answer: if the diviner himself creates 80
and contrives the events which he announces in advance.

It was all very well for the Jewish prophets to prophesy that

1 [Part II of "The Strife of the Faculties." See Introduction, p. xi and note 5.]

2 From Pythia to the gipsy girl, whoever dabbles in divination (doing it without knowledge or honesty) is said to be a *soothsayer*. [Pythia was Apollo's priestess at Delphi.]

sooner or later not simply decadence but complete dissolution awaited their state, for they themselves were the authors of this fate. As national leaders they had loaded their constitution with so much ecclesiastical freight, and civil freight tied to it, that their state became utterly unfit to subsist of itself, and especially unfit to subsist together with neighboring nations. Hence the jeremiads of their priests were naturally bound to be lost upon the winds, because the priests obstinately persisted in their design for an untenable constitution created by themselves; and thus they could infallibly foresee the issue.

So far as their influence extends, our politicians do precisely the same thing and are just as lucky in their prophecies. We must, they say, take men as they are, not as pedants ignorant of the world or good-natured visionaries fancy they ought to be. But in place of that "as they are" it would be better to say what they "have made" them—stubborn and inclined to revolt —through unjust constraint, through perfidious plots placed in the hands of the government; obviously then, if the government allows the reins to relax a little, sad consequences ensue which verify the prophecy of those supposedly sagacious statesmen.

Ecclesiastics, too, occasionally prophesy the complete destruction of religion and the imminent appearance of Antichrist; and in doing so they are performing precisely what is requisite to call him up. This happens because they have not seen to impressing on their parishes moral principles which lead directly to the better, but rather fabricate into essential duty observances and historical beliefs which are supposed to effect it indirectly; from this, of course, can grow the mechanical unanimity as in a civil constitution, but none in moral disposition. But then they complain about irreligion, which they themselves have caused and thus could predict even without any special prophetic talent.

3. CLASSIFICATION OF THE CONCEPT OF THAT WHICH WE WISH TO FOREKNOW AS REGARDS THE FUTURE

In three cases one could make predictions. The human race exists either in continual retrogression toward wickedness, or in perpetual progression toward improvement in its moral destination, or in eternal stagnation in its present stage of moral worth among creatures (a stagnation with which eternal rotation in orbit around the same point is one and the same).

The first assertion we can call moral terrorism, and the second eudaemonism (which could also be called chiliasm if we view the goal of progress within a broad prospectus); but the third we can term abderitism [3] because, since a true stagnation in matters of morality is not possible, a perpetually changing upward tendency and an equally frequent and profound relapse (an eternal oscillation, as it were) amounts to nothing more than if the subject had remained in the same place, standing still.

a) *Concerning the terroristic manner of representing human history*

Decline into wickedness cannot be incessant in the human race, for at a certain stage of disintegration it would destroy itself. Hence in connection with the increase of great atrocities looming up like mountains, and evils commensurate with them, it is said: now things cannot grow worse; Doomsday is at our doorstep; and the pious enthusiast by this time is already

3 [*Sc.* Abdera, center of the Atomic School of philosophy in the ancient world. Beside the metaphors which suggest the philosophy of Democritus, Kant may also have had in mind the ancient canard that the air of Abdera makes men silly. Wieland's *Die Geschichte der Abderiten* (1774), a popular satire comparing modern Biberach with ancient Abdera in point of silliness, made the name readily understandable to Kant's readers.]

dreaming of the restoration of all things and a renovated world after the time that this one will have perished in flames.

b) *Concerning the eudaemonistic manner of representing human history*

It may always be conceded that the proportion of good and evil elements inherent in our predisposition remains constant and can be neither augmented nor diminished in the same individual; how then should the quantity of good in our predisposition increase? For that would happen only through the freedom of the subject, for which purpose the subject would in turn require a greater reservoir of good than it now possesses. The effects cannot surpass the power of the efficient cause; thus the quantity of good mixed in man with the evil cannot exceed a certain measure beyond which it would be able to work its way up and thus ever proceed toward the better. Eudaemonism, with its sanguine hopes, therefore, appears to be untenable and to promise little in a prophetic history of humanity in favor of progress endlessly broadening its course toward the good.

c) *Concerning the abderitic hypothesis of the human race for the predetermination of its history*

This opinion may well have the majority of voices on its side. Bustling folly is the character of our species: people hastily set off on the path of the good, but do not persevere steadfastly upon it; indeed, in order to avoid being bound to a single goal, even if only for the sake of variety they reverse the plan of progress, build in order to demolish, and impose upon themselves the hopeless effort of rolling the stone of Sisyphus uphill in order to let it roll back down again. The principle of evil in the natural predisposition of the human race, therefore, does not seem to be amalgamated (blended) here with that of the good, but each principle appears rather to be neutralized by the other. Inertia (which is called here stagnation) would be the result of this. It is a vain affair to have good so alternate with evil that the whole traffic of our species with itself on this globe would have to be considered as a mere farcical comedy, for this can endow our species with no greater value in the eyes of reason than that which other animal species possess, species which carry on this game with fewer costs and without expenditure of thought.

4. THE PROBLEM OF PROGRESS IS NOT TO BE RESOLVED DIRECTLY THROUGH EXPERIENCE   83

Even if we felt that the human race, considered as a whole, was to be conceived as progressing and proceeding forward for however long a time, still no one can guarantee that now, this very moment, with regard to the physical disposition of our species, the epoch of its decline would not be liable to occur; and inversely, if it is moving backwards, and in an accelerated fall into baseness, a person may not despair even then of encountering a juncture (*punctum flexus contrarii*) where the moral predisposition in our race would be able to turn anew toward the better. For we are dealing with beings that act freely, to whom, it is true, what they ought to do may be dictated in advance, but of whom it may not be predicted what they will do: we are dealing with beings who, from the feeling of self-inflicted evil, when things disintegrate altogether, know how to adopt a strengthened motive for making them even better than they were before that state. But "miserable mortals," says the Abbot Coyer,[4] "nothing is constant in your lives except inconstancy!"

If the course of human affairs seems so senseless to us, perhaps it lies in a poor choice of position from which we regard it. Viewed from the earth, the planets sometimes move backwards, sometimes forward, and sometimes not at all. But if the standpoint selected is the sun, an act which only reason can perform, according to the Copernican hypothesis they move constantly in their regular course. Some people, however, who

4 [Cf. p. 80 above, note 13.]

in other respects are not stupid, like to persist obstinately in their way of explaining the phenomena and in the point of view which they have once adopted, even if they should thereby entangle themselves to the point of absurdity in Tychonic cycles and epicycles.[5] But, and this is precisely the misfortune, we are not capable of placing ourselves in this position when it is a question of the prediction of free actions. For that would be the standpoint of Providence which is situated beyond all human wisdom, and which likewise extends to the free actions of man; these actions, of course, man can *see*, but not *foresee* with certitude (for the divine eye there is no distinction in this matter); because, in the final analysis, man requires coherency according to natural laws, but with respect to his future free actions he must dispense with this guidance or direction.

If we were able to attribute to man an inherent and unalterably good, albeit limited, will, he would be able to predict with certainty the progress of his species toward the better, because it would concern an event that he himself could produce. But in connection with the mixture of good and evil in his predisposition, the proportion of which he is incognizant, he himself does not know what effect he might expect from it.

5. YET THE PROPHETIC HISTORY OF THE HUMAN RACE MUST BE CONNECTED TO SOME EXPERIENCE

There must be some experience in the human race which, as an event, points to the disposition and capacity of the human race to be the cause of its own advance toward the better, and (since this should be the act of a being endowed with freedom),

[5] [Refers to the Danish astronomer, Tycho Brahe (1546-1601), who sought a *via media* between the Ptolemaic and Copernican systems by advancing the theory in his work, *Astronomiae Instauratae Progymnasmata*, Vol. II (1588), that the five planets then known, excluding earth, revolve around the sun, but the sun and solar system simultaneously revolve about the earth once annually.]

toward the human race as being the author of this advance. But from a given cause an event as an effect can be predicted [only] if the circumstances prevail which contribute to it. That these conditions must come to pass some time or other can, of course, be predicted in general, as in the calculation of probability in games of chance; but that prediction cannot enable us to know whether what is predicted is to happen in my life and I am to have the experience of it. Therefore, an event must be sought which points to the existence of such a cause and to its effectiveness in the human race, undetermined with regard to time, and which would allow progress toward the better to be concluded as an inevitable consequence. This conclusion then could also be extended to the history of the past (that it has always been in progress) in such a way that that event would have to be considered not itself as the cause of history, but only as an intimation, an historical sign (*signum rememorativum, demonstrativum, prognostikon*) demonstrating the tendency of the human race viewed in its entirety, that is, seen not as [a sum of] individuals (for that would yield an interminable enumeration and computation), but rather as divided into nations and states (as it is encountered on earth).

6. CONCERNING AN EVENT OF OUR TIME WHICH DEMONSTRATES THIS MORAL TENDENCY OF THE HUMAN RACE   85

This event consists neither in momentous deeds nor crimes committed by men whereby what was great among men is made small or what was small is made great, nor in ancient splendid political structures which vanish as if by magic while others come forth in their place as if from the depths of the earth. No, nothing of the sort. It is simply the mode of thinking of the spectators which reveals itself publicly in this game of great revolutions, and manifests such a universal yet disinterested sympathy for the players on one side against those on the other, even at the risk that this partiality could become very disadvantageous for them if discovered. Owing to its universality, this mode of thinking demonstrates a character of the human race at large and all at once; owing to its disinterestedness, a moral character of humanity, at least in its predisposition, a character which not only permits people to hope for progress toward the better, but is already itself progress insofar as its capacity is sufficient for the present.

The revolution [6] of a gifted people which we have seen unfolding in our day may succeed or miscarry; it may be filled with misery and atrocities to the point that a sensible man, were he boldly to hope to execute it successfully the second time, would never resolve to make the experiment at such cost —this revolution, I say, nonetheless finds in the hearts of all spectators (who are not engaged in this game themselves) a wishful participation that borders closely on enthusiasm, the very expression of which is fraught with danger; this sympathy, therefore, can have no other cause than a moral predisposition in the human race.

This moral cause inserting itself [in the course of events] is twofold: first, that of the *right,* that a nation must not be hindered in providing itself with a civil constitution, which appears good to the people themselves; and second, that of the *end* (which is, at the same time, a duty), that that same national constitution alone be just and morally good in itself, created in such a way as to avoid, by its very nature, principles permitting offensive war. It can be no other than a republican constitution, republican at least in essence; [7] it thus establishes

86

[6] [French Revolution. See Introduction, p. xii.]

[7] But this is not to say that a nation which has a monarchical constitution should therewith usurp the law, nor even only cherish the secret wish of seeing it changed; for its position in Europe, perhaps very extended, can recommend that constitution as the only one by which that nation can maintain itself among powerful neighbors. Likewise the grumbling of the subjects, provoked not by the internal policy of the government but by the conduct of the latter toward foreigners, if perchance that conduct should hinder the subjects in their republican tendencies, is no proof at all of the nation's dissatisfaction with its own constitution, but rather of love for it; because the nation is the more assured against any danger the more other nations pursue a republican policy.

the condition whereby war (the source of all evil and corruption of morals) is deterred; and, at least negatively, progress toward the better is assured humanity in spite of all its infirmity, for it is at least left undisturbed in its advance.

This, then, plus the passionate participation in the good, i.e., enthusiasm (although not to be wholly esteemed, since passion as such deserves censure), provide through this history the occasion for the following remark which is important for anthropology: genuine enthusiasm always moves only toward what is ideal and, indeed, to what is purely moral, such as the concept of right, and it cannot be grafted onto self-interest. Monetary rewards will not elevate the adversaries of the revolution to the zeal and grandeur of soul which the pure concept of right produced in them; and even the concept of honor among the old martial nobility (an analogue to enthusiasm) vanished before the weapons of those who kept in view [8] the

---

Nevertheless, some slanderous sycophants, to make themselves important, have sought to pass off this innocuous political twaddle as fondness for innovation, Jacobinism and mob action which would threaten the state; yet, under the circumstances, there was not even the least reason for these allegations, particularly in a country more than a hundred miles removed from the scene of the revolution.

[8] Of such an enthusiasm for upholding justice for the human race we can say: "postquam ad arma Vulcania ventum est, mortalis mucro glacies ceu futilis ictu dissiluit." * Why has a ruler never dared openly to declare that he recognizes absolutely no right of the people opposed to him, that his people owe their happiness solely to the beneficence of a government which confers this happiness upon them, and that all presumption of the subject to a right opposed to the government (since this right comprehends the concept of permissible resistance) is absurd and even culpable? The reason is that such a public declaration would rouse all of his subjects against him; although, as docile sheep, led by a benevolent and sensible master, well-fed and powerfully protected, they would have nothing wanting in their welfare for which to lament. For a being endowed with freedom is not satisfied with the pleasure of life's comforts which fall to his lot by the act of another (in this case the government); what matters rather is the principle according to which the individual provides such things for himself. But welfare possesses no principle either for him who receives it or for him who dispenses it (one places it here, the other there), inasmuch as what matters in wel-

right of the nation to which they belonged and of which they considered themselves the guardians; with what exaltation the uninvolved public looking on sympathized then without the

87   least intention of assisting.

7. PROPHETIC HISTORY OF HUMANITY

In the principle there must be something moral, which reason presents as pure; but because of its great and epoch-making influence, reason must present it as the acknowledged duty of the human soul, concerning mankind as a whole (*non singularum, sed universorum*), which hails, with such universal and impartial sympathy, the hopes for its success and the efforts toward realizing it. This even is the phenomenon, not of revolution, but (as Erhard expresses it) [9] a phenomenon of the evolution of a constitution in accordance with natural law which, to be sure, is still not won solely by desperate battles—

88   for war, both civil and foreign, destroys all previously existing

---

fare is the material of the will, which is empirical, and which is thus unfit for the universality of a rule. A being endowed with freedom, in the consciousness of his superiority over the irrational animal, can and should, therefore, according to the formal principle of his will, demand no other government for the people to which he belongs than one in which the people are co-legislative; that is, the right of men who are supposed to obey must necessarily precede all regard for well-being, and this right is a blessing that is exalted above all price (of utility), and one upon which no government, however beneficent it may persistently be, is permitted to infringe. But this right is still always only an Idea of which the realization is restricted to the condition of accord of its means with the morality which the nation may not transgress; and this may not come to pass through revolution which is always unjust. To rule autocratically and yet to govern in a republican way, that is, in the spirit of republicanism and on an analogy with it—that is what makes a nation satisfied with its constitution.

* ["When it met the divine Vulcanian armour, the mortal blade, like brittle ice, snapped in the stroke. . . ." Refers to Meliscus' sword, the weapon Aeneas snatched in his battle with Turnus. (Virgil, *Aeneid* XII. 739f., trans. J. W. Mackail, "Modern Library" edn.)]

9 [Kant's reference is to a work of Johann B. Erhard (1766-1827), *Über das Recht des Volkes zu einer Revolution* (Jena and Leipzig, 1795), p. 189.]

statutory constitutions. This evolution leads to striving after a constitution that cannot be bellicose, that is to say, a republican constitution. The constitution may be republican either in its *political form* or only in its *manner of governing,* in having the state ruled through the unity of the sovereign (the monarch) by analogy with the laws that a nation would provide itself in accordance with the universal principles of legality.

Now I claim to be able to predict to the human race—even without prophetic insight—according to the aspects and omens of our day, the attainment of this goal. That is, I predict its progress toward the better which, from now on, turns out to be no longer completely retrogressive. For such a phenomenon in human history *is not to be forgotten,* because it has revealed a tendency and faculty in human nature for improvement such that no politician, affecting wisdom, might have conjured out of the course of things hitherto existing, and one which nature and freedom alone, united in the human race in conformity with inner principles of right, could have promised. But so far as time is concerned, it can promise this only indefinitely and as a contingent event.

But even if the end viewed in connection with this event should not now be attained, even if the revolution or reform of a national constitution should finally miscarry, or, after some time had elapsed, everything should relapse into its former rut (as politicians now predict), that philosophical prophesy still would lose nothing of its force. For that event is too important, too much interwoven with the interest of humanity, and its influence too widely propagated in all areas of the world to not be recalled on any favorable occasion by the nations which would then be roused to a repetition of new efforts of this kind; because then, in an affair so important for humanity, the intended constitution, at a certain time, must finally attain that constancy which instruction by repeated experience suffices to establish in the the minds of all men.

Here, therefore, is a proposition valid for the most rigorous theory, in spite of all skeptics, and not just a well-meaning and practically commendable proposition: The human race has

always been in progress toward the better and will continue to
89   be so henceforth. To him who does not consider what happens
in just some one nation but also has regard to the whole scope
of all the peoples on earth who will gradually come to partici-
pate in progress, this reveals the prospect of an immeasurable
time—provided at least that there does not, by some chance,
occur a second epoch of natural revolution which will push
aside the human race to clear the stage for other creatures, like
that which (according to Camper and Blumenbach [10]) sub-
merged the plant and animal kingdoms before men ever existed. For in the face of the omnipotence of nature, or rather
its supreme first cause which is inaccessible to us, the human
being is, in his turn, but a trifle. But for the sovereigns of his
own species also to consider and treat him as such, whether by
burdening him as an animal, regarding him as a mere tool of
their designs, or exposing him in their conflicts with one another in order to have him massacred—that is no trifle, but a
subversion of the ultimate purpose of creation itself.

8. CONCERNING THE DIFFICULTY OF THE
MAXIMS APPLYING TO WORLD PROGRESS
WITH REGARD TO THEIR PUBLICITY

Enlightenment of the masses is the public instruction of the
people in its duties and rights vis-à-vis the state to which they
belong. Since only natural rights and rights arising out of the
common human understanding are concerned here, then the
natural heralds and expositors of these among the people are
not officially appointed by the state but are free professors of
law, that is philosophers who, precisely because this freedom
is allowed to them, are objectionable to the state, which always
desires to rule alone; and they are decried, under the name of
enlighteners, as persons dangerous to the state, although their

---

[10] [Kant's references are to the work of Petrus Camper (1722-89), *Über
den natürlichen Unterschied der Gesichtszüge* (Berlin, 1792), and to the
Handbuch der Naturgeschichte (Göttingen, 1779) by Johann F. Blumenbach (1752-1840).]

voice is not addressed confidentially to the people (as the people take scarcely any or no notice at all of it and of their writings) but is addressed respectfully to the state; and they implore the state to take to heart that need which is felt to be legitimate. This can happen by no other means than that of publicity in the event that an entire people cares to bring forward its grievances (gravamen). Thus the prohibition of publicity impedes the progress of a people toward improvement, even in that which applies to the least of its claims, namely its simple, natural right.

Another disguise, which is easily penetrated indeed, but is   90
one to which a nation, nevertheless, is legally committed, is that pertaining to the true nature of its constitution. It would be an insult to its majesty to say of the British nation that it is an absolute monarchy: some rather maintain that a constitution limiting the will of the monarch through the two Houses of Parliament, acting as representatives of the people, is supposed to exist; and yet everyone knows perfectly well that the monarch's influence on these representatives is so great and so certain that nothing is resolved by the Houses except what he wills and purposes through his minister. The latter then probably even proposes resolutions in connection with which he knows that he will be contradicted, and even arranges it that way (for example, with regard to slave-trade) in order to provide a fictitious proof of the freedom of Parliament. This representation of the nature of the case has something delusive about it so that the true constitution, faithful to law, is no longer sought at all; for a person imagines he has found it in an example already at hand, and a false publicity deceives the people with the illusion of a limited monarchy [11] in power by

[11] A cause, the nature of which one does directly understand, makes itself known through the effect which unfailingly attaches to it. What is an *absolute* monarch? He is one at whose command, if he says, "war is necessary," a state of war immediately exists. What is a *limited* monarch, on the other hand? He who must first consult the people as to whether war is or is not to be; and the people say, "there is to be no war," so there is no war. For war is a situation in which *all* political power must be at the disposal of the sovereign. Now the British monarch

a law which issues from them, while their representitives, won over by bribery, have secretly subjected them to an absolute monarchy.

91   The Idea of a constitution in harmony with the natural right of man, one namely in which the citizens obedient to the law, besides being united, ought also to be legislative, lies at the basis of all political forms; and the body politic which, conceived in conformity to it by virtue of pure concepts of reason, signifies a Platonic Ideal (*respublica noumenon*), is not an empty chimera, but rather the eternal norm for all civil organization in general, and averts all war. A civil society organized conformably to this ideal is the representation of it in agreement with the laws of freedom by means of an example in our experience (*respublica phaenomenon*) and can only be painfully acquired after multifarious hostilities and wars; but its constitution, once won on a large scale, is qualified as the best among all others to banish war, the destroyer of everything good. Consequently, it is a duty to enter into such a system of government, but it is provisionally the duty of the monarchs, if they rule as autocrats, to govern in a republican (not democratic) way, that is, to treat the people according to principles which are commensurate with the spirit of libertarian laws (as a nation with mature understanding would prescribe them for itself), although they would not be literally canvassed for their consent.

---

has conducted wars aplenty without seeking the consent for them. Therefore, this king is an absolute monarch who ought not to be one, of course, according to the constitution; but he is always able to bypass it because precisely through those political powers, namely, that he has it in his power to dispense all appointments and posts, he can consider assured the assent of the representatives of the people. In order to succeed, however, this system of bribery must certainly not be publicized. Hence it remains under the highly transparent veil of secrecy.

9. WHAT PROFIT WILL PROGRESS TOWARD THE BETTER YIELD HUMANITY?

Not an ever-growing quantity of morality with regard to intention, but an increase of the products of legality in dutiful actions whatever their motives. That is, the profit (result) of man's striving toward the better can be assumed to reside alone in the good deeds of men, which will become better and better and more and more numerous; it resides alone in phenomena constituting the moral state of the human race. For we have only empirical data (experiences) upon which we are founding this prediction, namely, the physical cause of our actions as these actually occur as phenomena; and not the moral cause— the only one which can be established purely a priori—which contains the concept of duty with respect to what ought to happen.

Gradually violence on the part of the powers will diminish and obedience to the laws will increase. There will arise in the body politic perhaps more charity and less strife in lawsuits, more reliability in keeping one's word, etc., partly out of love of honor, partly out of well-understood self-interest. And eventually this will also extend to nations in their external relations   92 toward one another up to the realization of the cosmopolitan society, without the moral foundation in mankind having to be enlarged in the least; for that, a kind of new creation (supernatural influence) would be necessary. For we must also not hope for too much from men in their progress toward the better lest we fall prey with good reason to the mockery of the politician who would willingly take the hope of man as the dreaming of a distraught mind.[12]

[12] It is sweet, however, to imagine constitutions corresponding to the requirements of reason (particularly in a legal sense), but rash to propose them and culpable to incite the populace to abolish what presently exists.

Plato's *Atlantica*, More's *Utopia*, Harrington's *Oceana* and Allais' *Severambia* have been successively brought on the scene, but have never so much as been tried (Cromwell's abortive monster of a despotic republic

10. IN WHAT ORDER ALONE CAN PROGRESS TOWARD THE BETTER BE EXPECTED?

The answer is: not by the movement of things *from bottom to top,* but *from top to bottom.* To expect not simply to train good citizens but good men who can improve and take care of themselves; to expect that this will eventually happen by means of education of youth in the home, then in schools on both the lowest and highest level, in intellectual and moral culture fortified by religious doctrine—that is desirable, but its success is hardly to be hoped for. For while the people feel
93 that the costs for education of their youth ought to be borne, not by them, but by the state, the state for its part has no money left (as Büsching complains) [13] for the salaries of its teachers who are capable and zealously devoted to their spheres of duty, since it uses all the money for war. Rather, the whole mechanism of this education has no coherence if it is not designed in agreement with a well-weighed plan of the sovereign power, put into play according to the purpose of this plan, and steadily maintained therein; to this end it might well behoove the state likewise to reform itself from time to time and, at-

---

excepted).* The same goes for political creations as for the creation of the world; no human was present there, nor could he have been present at such an event, since he must have been his own creator otherwise. However late it may be, to hope someday for the consummation of a political product, as it is envisaged here, is a sweet dream; but that it is being perpetually approached is not only *thinkable,* but, so far as it is compatible with the moral law, an *obligation,* not of the citizens, but of the sovereign.

* [Sir Thomas More's political satire was published in 1516 in Latin, was translated into English in 1551. The *Oceana* contained Harrington's exposition of an ideal constitution, the lawgiver supposedly Oliver Cromwell, whose protectorate over England lasted from 1653-58. The *Histoire des Severambes* appeared first in English, 1675, then in French, 1677 and 1679, and is supposed to derive from a certain Vairasse d'Allais.]

[13] [Anton F. Büsching (1724-93) was the author of extensive writings on geography, history, education and religion, as well as the editor of the *Magazin für die neue Historie und Geographie* (23 vols., 1767-93) and *Wochentl. Nachrichten von neuen Landkarten* (Berlin, 1773-87).]

tempting evolution instead of revolution, progress perpetually toward the better. Nevertheless, since they are also human beings who must effect this education, consequently such beings who themselves have to be trained for that purpose, then, considering this infirmity of human nature as subject to the contingency of events which favor such an effect, the hope for its progress is to be expected only on the condition of a wisdom from above (which bears the name of Providence if it is invisible to us); but for that which can be expected and exacted from *men* in this area toward the advancement of this aim, we can anticipate only a negative wisdom, namely, that they will see themselves compelled to render the greatest obstacle to morality—that is to say war, which constantly retards this advancement—firstly by degrees more humane and then rarer, and finally to renounce offensive war altogether, in order to enter upon a constitution which by its nature and without loss of power is founded on genuine principles of right, and which can persistently progress toward the better.

CONCLUSION

A doctor who consoled his patients from one day to the next with hopes of a speedy convalescence, pledging to one that his pulse beat better, to another an improvement in his stool, to a third the same regarding his perspiration, etc., received a visit from one of his friends. "How's your illness, my friend," was his first question. "How should it be? I'm dying of improvement, pure and simple!" I blame no one when, considering the ills of the state, he begins to despair of the health of humanity and its progress toward the better; but I would rely on the heroic remedy which Hume prescribes and which would effect a quick cure. "If, at the present time," he says, "I see the nations on the point of war with one another, it is as if I were seeing two besotted fellows beating each other about with cudgels in a china shop. For not only do they have to recover slowly from the bruises they administered to each other, but afterwards they must pay for the damages that they have

done." [14] *Sero sapiunt Phryges.*[15] However, the painful consequences of the present war can compel the political prophet
to confess a very imminent turn of humanity toward the better
that is even now in prospect.

[14] [Hume wrote: "I must confess, when I see princes and states fighting
and quarrelling, amidst their debts, funds, and public mortgages, it
always brings to my mind a match of cudgel-playing fought in a China
shop." "Of Public Credit," in *Essays, Moral, Political and Literary,* eds.
Green and Grose (London, 1898). The "heroic remedy" Hume refers to
is the refusal to support war through contracting public debts. Kant
proposed the same in *Perpetual Peace,* see above, p. 88.]

[15] ["The Phrygians are wise too late" (Cicero, *ad fam.* VII. 16).]